Third Edition

GUIDELINES

A Cross-Cultural Reading / Writing Text

TEACHER'S MANUAL

RUTH SPACK

CAMBRIDGE
UNIVERSITY PRESS

32 Avenue of the Americas, New York NY 10013-2473, USA

Cambridge University Press is part of the University of Cambridge.

It furthers the University's mission by disseminating knowledge in the pursuit of education, learning and research at the highest international levels of excellence.

www.cambridge.org
Information on this title: www.cambridge.org/9780521613026

First published 2007
2nd printing 2008

A catalogue record for this publication is available from the British Library

ISBN 978-0-521-61302-6 Paperback

CONTENTS

INTRODUCTION

Guidelines has grown out of my own teaching experiences. What appears in the text is the result of years of experimenting in the classroom as I tried out new readings, writing assignments, and approaches. For that reason, I do not expect any instructor to use all of the material in this text in one semester. Nor do I expect anyone to use only the material in this book. My goal is to present a versatile text that allows instructors to select whatever seems most productive and to add or substitute other readings and assignments that enrich students' experiences in and out of the classroom.

I expect and hope, too, that instructors will not feel compelled to follow the order of the text. Common themes resonate across readings and writing assignments, making it possible for a reading in one chapter to be used for a writing assignment in another, and vice versa. For me, the long-term success of *Guidelines* is reflected in the work of the hundreds of instructors who, over the years, have treated the book as a springboard for the creation of their own imaginative and intellectually challenging curricula for the purpose of involving students in authentic and meaningful work and thus facilitating their acquisition of language and literacy.

Guidelines is based on the idea that students' academic writing can improve dramatically if the following conditions are met:
- Students have regular, substantial, and purposeful practice in reading and writing a variety of texts.
- Students are made aware of varying purposes for reading and writing.
- Students are provided with meaningful examples of reading and writing.
- Students are exposed to the processes of other readers and writers at work.
- Students receive timely, positive, and constructive feedback on their work in progress.
- Students have time to generate, draft, organize, and revise ideas.

I welcome feedback on this third edition. Please feel free to contact me with questions, critiques, new ideas, or samples of students' writing in response to the book's tasks and assignments: rspack@bentley.edu.

Contents and Structure of the Third Edition

This new edition of *Guidelines* incorporates feedback from numerous students, instructors, reviewers, and editors who have used or evaluated previous editions. It retains the features that are most appreciated, including the integration of reading and writing, a generous selection of diverse and thought-provoking readings, pre-reading and post-reading activities that encourage students to interact with what they read, a variety of tasks that motivate and enable students to write, strategies for fulfilling specific essay and research assignments, guidelines boxes that present writing instruction in a format that is easy to understand and use, illustrative examples of student writers at work, and a learner-centered philosophy that encourages students to write from their own perspectives as they analyze and interpret what they read.

Within that context, I have made a number of significant revisions. To freshen and update the book, I have omitted eight readings and added seven new ones. I have also added a new student research essay that incorporates Web-based research. In place of the poetry unit, I have created a chapter that includes an assignment to relate reading to experience, which provides a relatively smooth transition from personal writing to writing from sources. All of the essay assignments are now more specific, with clearer instructions, and are paired with checklists that provide corresponding evaluative criteria. The entire text has been reorganized for the purpose of clarity and accessibility, including a separate handbook for writing, and there are clearer guidelines overall. Other changes are outlined in the following explanations of each part of the book.

▨ Part One: *Responding to Reading*

Part One consists of one chapter, Strategies for Reading Critically, which provides a variety of approaches to help students strengthen their ability to read critically. New to this chapter are guidelines for clustering ideas from a reading and for taking notes on a reading.

▨ Part Two: *Readings and Writing Assignments*

Readings in Part Two are now organized according to specific essay assignments, rather than according to genre: Writing from Experience, Relating Reading to Experience, Analyzing an Argumentative Essay, and Analyzing Fiction. Also new to Part Two are individual discussion activities for each reading selection.

▨ Part Three: *Research and Writing Assignments*

This new Part Three brings together two research chapters, Writing from Field Research and Writing from Library and Web-Based Research, and includes updated guidelines for online research.

▨ A Handbook for Writing

The new handbook includes guidelines for citing, incorporating, and documenting sources; guidelines for drafting, exchanging feedback on, and revising essays; and guidelines for locating and correcting errors. The handbook is designed to be used as a resource in conjunction with the essay assignments in Parts Two and Three.

Content and Structure of the Chapters

Chapter 1 includes three readings and corresponding reading tasks, with several suggestions for using writing to discover meaning in a text and to generate ideas. Chapters 2 through 5 each begin with four or five readings that are followed by guidelines designed to help students fulfill the chapter's corresponding essay assignment. Chapters 6 and 7 consist of guidelines for fulfilling each chapter's respective research assignment.

Readings

All of the readings in *Guidelines* have received strong responses in my classes and thus have led to interesting class discussions. I find that a class is most successful when students see that their ideas are valued, that there is not one correct response, and that multiple perspectives can be brought to bear on the readings. At the same time, I encourage close reading so that the class does not perpetuate ideas or facts that are not true to the text.

The three reading selections in Chapter 1, Strategies for Reading Critically, provide sources to which students can apply numerous guidelines for reading critically. These readings anticipate some of the larger themes that emerge in subsequent chapters, including teaching and learning, living in multiple worlds, communicating across languages and cultures, and acquiring new ways to gain knowledge.

The five reading selections in Chapter 2, Writing from Experience, demonstrate a variety of ways to convey an insight or express a viewpoint that grows out of personal experience. Written by authors who have lived in multiple worlds, these readings convey what it actually means to acquire new ways of living and communicating across languages and cultures.

The four reading selections in Chapter 3, Relating Reading to Experience, including three research studies, can become sources for students' own essays as they test an author's ideas against their own experiences. These readings address issues related to communicating across languages and cultures and adapting to new approaches to learning and literacy.

The five reading selections in Chapter 4, Analyzing an Argumentative Essay, can become sources for students' own essays as they determine the strengths and weaknesses of an author's argument. The authors of these essays tackle controversial issues related to education: what students should be taught, how they should be taught, and how their learning should be assessed.

The five reading selections in Chapter 5, Analyzing Fiction, can become sources for students' own essays as they analyze a short story to develop an interpretation that grows out of the details of the work. Spanning more than 100 years, these fictional pieces reflect some of the problems and possibilities of living in the United States as the authors take readers inside the minds of their characters to show what it means for them to live as slaves, immigrants, or exiles.

Each chapter of readings in *Guidelines* is informed by a particular theme and assignment, but common themes and writing possibilities resonate across the chapters. For example, the readings in Chapter 2 can be used with the essay assignment in Chapter 3. Alternatively, students can synthesize readings from two or more chapters, drawing ideas and examples for their own writing from a variety of genres: personal essays, research studies, argumentative essays, and short stories.

In this Teacher's Manual, I summarize each of the readings in *Guidelines*, but these summaries do not represent the final word on the essence of a particular selection.

A thematic arrangement of the readings can be found on page 57 of this manual.

▨ Accompanying the Readings

Each reading is accompanied by three tasks: a pre-reading task that asks students to reflect in writing on the title or topic of the reading, a post-reading writing task that asks students to reflect on and briefly summarize what they have just read, and a post-reading discussion task.

Write Before You Read

Preceding most of the readings in *Guidelines* is a Write Before You Read activity that directs students to write about the title or content of the selection they are about to read. If there is time, I ask students to write at the end of a class period, before the assigned reading is due, and we discuss their responses in order to construct shared knowledge about the subject matter. If there is no time for in-class writing, I ask them to write a response outside of class or just to think about the topic. This activity is designed to stimulate interest in the reading and, ideally, to facilitate comprehension. Students can compare their own texts with the professional texts and analyze similarities and differences in content and style. This process has the added benefit of helping students develop a deeper understanding of how language can be used both to create and to comprehend a written text.

Write After You Read

The Write After You Read instructions that follow each reading in *Guidelines* ask students to make a journal entry on the reading and to summarize the reading in one or two sentences. The journal guidelines, which appear in Chapter 1 on page 11, tell students that they may write whatever they want in response to the reading or follow one or more suggestions, which range from exploring what interested or confused them to answering the Discuss After You Read questions. Students usually write the summaries of the readings in their journal entries. Students' responses in their journal entries are the springboard for class discussions, and the summaries become part of the class discussion when a student volunteer shares a written summary or just summarizes orally, and other students join in to provide what they perceive to be a more accurate or complete account. Summaries differ, of course, and by looking at or hearing each other's summaries, students can come to see that readers focus on different aspects of a reading for different reasons and purposes. Although my aim is not to come up with the "right" answer, I am careful to filter out inaccuracies; and often students do agree on the essence of a reading.

Discuss After You Read

The Discuss After You Read questions are designed to guide students to analyze the text in some depth. My experience has been that students may have significantly different responses to any given reading. Some students may identify with a writer while others may disagree with a writer's philosophy. I first ask students to share their initial reactions to what they have read. Often that is all that is needed to get the discussion going and continuing for quite a while. Sometimes I ask each student to share a journal response; other times a few students respond and then others join in. My goal is for most students to contribute before the discussion of the reading ends. I try to do as little talking as possible so that students are the ones who raise questions, read aloud, and explain baffling passages to one another. Students have a tendency to direct their comments to me even when they are responding to or challenging another student's comment. Since I want students to interact with one another, I look at the student who just spoke while the next student is speaking. Ideally, that causes the second student to turn and speak to the first student rather than to speak directly to me. Then – if it works – the two students talk to each other.

Guidelines

Each chapter includes guidelines to help students strengthen their reading or writing. These guidelines are meant to be just that: guidelines – not rigid formulas that students must follow. The guidelines in Chapters 2 through 7 explain different ways to explore a topic; to focus ideas; and to develop a structure for the assigned essay in that chapter, illustrated by a corresponding flow chart. At the end of each chapter, students are presented with a checklist that provides evaluative criteria for that particular essay.

Guidelines in Part One: Responding to Reading
Part One includes guidelines for students to make predictions about a reading's content, develop reading fluency, closely examine an author's ideas and experiences, and capture their own reactions to those ideas and experiences.

Guidelines in Part Two: Readings and Writing Assignments
Part Two includes guidelines for students to fulfill assignments to write from experience, relate reading to experience, analyze an argumentative essay, and analyze fiction.

Guidelines in Part Three: Research and Writing Assignments
Part Three includes guidelines for students to fulfill assignments written from field research and from library and Web-based research.

Guidelines in A Handbook for Writing
A Handbook for Writing includes guidelines for students to cite, incorporate, and document sources; to draft, to exchange feedback, and to revise; and to locate and correct errors.

▨ Accompanying the Guidelines

The Guidelines sections provide a considerable amount of guidance to help students fulfill the specific assignment for the chapter. Students are invited to examine how other students have engaged with the processes outlined in the guidelines. They are then asked to apply the guidelines to their own work and to analyze sample writings.

A student reader at work / A student writer at work

A unique feature of *Guidelines* is the opportunity for students to observe examples of how other students have undertaken the reading and writing tasks assigned in the book.

Your turn

Having observed how other student readers and writers have worked through the guidelines, students are invited to apply the guidelines to their own reading and writing. An arrow in the margin of the text directs students' attention to these tasks.

Activity

Numerous activities engage students in the processes of reading critically and summarizing, paraphrasing, quoting, synthesizing, documenting, and analyzing or correcting examples of professional and student writing. Further activities direct students to exchange feedback on each other's writing, proofread their own writing, examine the causes of their own errors, and edit their own texts. An arrow in the margin of the text directs students' attention to these activities.

Reflections on Teaching Writing

I always experiment with different approaches in my classes and then reflect on the effectiveness of the new strategies. Over the years, for example, my approaches to assigning journals, conducting conferences, and grading student writing have undergone change. I also periodically change the order of the essay assignments presented in *Guidelines*, combine chapters, or organize the material according to thematic categories rather than essay assignments. For examples of different ways to assign the material in *Guidelines*, see "Planning a Writing Course" in this Teacher's Manual (pages 51–56).

▨ Student Journal Writing and Teacher Journal Writing

The journal project on pages 10–12 primarily entails students' capturing their responses to the course readings. Often, though, I encourage students to write about their own writing as well, for example by asking them to discuss how they might go about fulfilling an essay assignment, how they did fulfill an assignment, or how they assess their own writing. I ask students to type each journal entry on a separate sheet of paper. I collect journal entries, which are typically two to three double-spaced pages, at the end of the class, comment on them, and return them at the beginning of the next class. Students later include these entries, with my comments, in their course portfolios.

Students may have difficulty understanding exactly what *journal* means if they have never kept this kind of journal before. Some may not fully understand what is expected of them until they have written and received feedback on one or two journal entries.

Over the years, I have experimented with several approaches, all successful, including the following:

- I ask students to write entries both in and out of class.
- I assign entries only as homework.
- I assign two entries a week, one for each class meeting.
- I assign one entry a week, with all students writing about the same reading or readings.
- I assign one entry a week but give students a choice of day on which to hand in an entry, with different readings assigned on the different days.
- I assign entries throughout the semester.
- I assign entries for one-half or three-quarters of the semester.

Whatever approach I have used, my pattern has been to respond positively to the content of each entry, identifying strong points, answering questions, expanding on a point, providing suggestions, or asking either clarifying questions or questions intended to challenge the student further. Most of my responses are in the margins. My end responses range in length from a few words to a paragraph, depending on my time allotment and on my reaction to what I have read. I do not grade the entries, although I do keep a record of them: I give the entries a number (Entry 1, Entry 2, and so on) and simply make a check in a roll book when they are handed in, noting if they are late. I expect students to hand in the assigned number of entries in order to pass the course. Online journals in which students respond to one another's writing provide an ongoing written interchange that reinforces their efforts, make it possible for students to consider their own interpretations in light of other readers' analyses, and enable them to draw on their own authority to respond back.

One of the great values of journal writing in my classes is the role it serves in fostering class discussion. The opportunity to shape ideas in writing before a class discussion allows students to rehearse and articulate their thoughts and thus enables their classroom participation.

I believe that individual grades on journal entries (such as A, B, C) are counterproductive, implying inappropriately that there are right and wrong responses. And I believe that correction of all errors on journal entries sends the wrong message: that error should be the central focus of writing. In fact, I rarely correct errors on the entries. If I correct at all, it is usually only to write the correct spelling above a word. I want students to learn early in the course that exploratory writing is valued, that taking risks to develop ideas is a worthy process. By responding to what students say rather than to the particulars of how they say it, I can convey interest in the students' viewpoints. If that interest carries over to the more formal essay assignments, students may be motivated to compose essays not only to do well in the course but also to communicate ideas.

Sometimes I keep a journal along with the students, responding to the course material and photocopying my entries to share with the class. By including excerpts from students' journal entries in my journal, I extend the interaction, which can lead to a more dynamic group awareness and exchange of ideas. Of course, the length and number of journal entries I write is dependent on the amount of time and energy I can devote to the project. (For further reading on this project, see *TESOL Quarterly*, December 1983, pp. 575–593, for an article I co-authored with Catherine Sadow titled, "Student-Teacher Working Journals in ESL Composition.")

Student-Instructor Individual and Group Conferences

I used to write detailed comments in the margins and at the end of students' drafts until a student pointed out that I had written more than she had! She may have been telling me that she appreciated the time and effort I had put in, but I started to think that there was something wrong with what I was doing. Wasn't the idea to have the students, not the instructor, do the writing? Now, instead of taking so much time responding to early drafts with lengthy written comments, I read them, write only brief positive comments ("good point"; "nicely expressed") in the margins, and then make a list of notes at the end, which are actually written primarily for myself, to remind me of what I want to cover when I meet with the student in a conference.

I typically begin the conference with the statement, "Tell me about the process you went through to write this draft." I then sit back and listen to what is often a revealing tale. In describing what they have done, many students actually reveal what they *intended* to do, not what they accomplished. They then realize that the paper may not reflect what they want it to, and we discuss how they can revise the paper to reflect their intentions. I keep a pen and lined notepad on my desk so that students can write down what they want to add to or change in their drafts. I feel a conference has been successful if a student does most of the talking and leaves with a paper full of self-generated ideas for revision. Such an approach provides students with the opportunity to stretch and grow as writers. Of course, I do speak in the conference, usually to ask questions, to answer the student's questions, to engage in a conversation about the course reading, and/or to share my initial reactions to what the student wrote. I give direct advice when I think it is appropriate. Some students need such instructional intervention in order to learn how to proceed. I also use some time to address language errors, especially those that interfere with comprehension, so that they won't be carried over into the revisions.

As an alternative to the one-on-one conference, I have found it valuable to meet in conference with small groups of students who have read each other's papers ahead of time and who have filled out a Feedback Form (page 277) for each paper. In the conference, we discuss one paper at a time. Students take turns explaining their papers and then listening to the students in their group as they provide positive feedback and constructive recommendations for revision. Ideally, students engage in conversation with each other about the strengths and weaknesses of their own writing. To promote that interaction, I take notes during the discussion – an approach that makes it necessary for students to talk to each other rather than to me. I occasionally guide the conversation, for example, by asking the writer how he or she might revise the paper in order to address a piece of criticism; but I let the students do most of the talking until every paper has been discussed. At that point, I raise any questions or add any insights that were not covered by the students themselves. I also take the opportunity to provide some overall writing instruction, which grows out of common features in the student drafts.

Toward the end of a conference, I hand students a yellow highlighter and ask them to do two tasks. First, I instruct them to underline the last sentence of their introduction. If they have trouble determining where their introduction ends – or if they have no introduction at all – I tell them that their readers will have trouble as well, and that is a sign that they need to revise the opening. Second, I instruct them to highlight the first sentence of every paragraph after the introduction until they come to the conclusion. They should now have a visual map of the ideas in their essays. Although there are exceptions, the idea in this first sentence should link what was just said in the previous paragraph to what is about to be said in the new paragraph, and the new paragraph should include details and quotations that serve to develop that idea. I look at the highlighted sentences with the students and help them decide if their sentences have fulfilled their expected tasks. Ideally, these first sentences show readers the thinking process of the writer and allow for a more fluid reading.

Grading Student Writing

I no longer grade individual papers. I agree with Peter Elbow, who argues that ranking individual papers is arbitrary and uninformative ("Ranking, Evaluating, and Liking: Sorting Out Three Forms of Judgment," *College English* 55.2, February 1993, pp. 187–206). I do express judgment of students' papers by commenting on their strengths and weaknesses, without having to justify a grade. I typically have short midterm conferences with individual students to discuss their portfolio of work (all of the writing they have done for the course, with my comments), which they bring to the conference; give them what I call "a ballpark figure" for a portfolio grade; and suggest what they can do to strengthen the portfolio, if needed. At the end of the semester, the whole class generates criteria for evaluation of the portfolio, and students evaluate their own portfolios accordingly. I then collect the portfolios and self-evaluations and grade the body of each student's work. The final course grade, then, reflects what the student has accomplished over time rather than only what the student has done or failed to do at any given moment.

RESPONDING TO READING

Part One presents various ways to respond to reading, with the aim of helping students develop strategies for reading critically.

Chapter 1
Strategies for Reading Critically

Chapter 1 focuses on developing effective reading strategies. The guidelines suggest ways for students to make predictions about a reading's content, foster their reading fluency, distinguish between the author's ideas and experiences and their own reactions to those ideas and experiences, and take a critical stance toward the text. Students can apply the chapter's guidelines to the three readings that are included in the chapter. Many of the strategies are based on the understanding that reading is neither a matter of understanding every word nor a simple process of locating a specific idea that resides in a text as a fixed concept. The act of reading shares with the act of writing an active engagement through which meaning is constructed. Both processes are characterized by the interaction of multiple factors, including the text itself and the reader's prior knowledge. When students bring their own perspectives to bear on the issues raised in the reading, they are able to enter the text, examine their preconceptions critically, and participate in the ongoing intellectual discussion about the subject matter.

GUIDELINES

The guidelines in this chapter introduce students to seven reading strategies: generating background knowledge, using clues to guess at meaning, annotating, clustering ideas, making double-entry notes, taking notes, and writing a journal entry on the reading. Many of these strategies involve writing because reading and writing contribute to each other in significant ways. Writing ability is strengthened through extensive reading for genuine interest or need, and reading ability is enhanced by writing activities that focus on exploring and generating meaning. When students learn to approach reading and writing as interactive ways to learn and to generate their own ideas, they are more likely to become better readers and writers.

Chapter Assignment (page 4)

The chapter assignment asks students to practice a variety of strategies designed to lead them to read critically. As students apply the chapter's guidelines to one or more of the reading selections in the chapter, they can share their reactions and ideas with a partner, in a small group, or with the whole class.

Depending on the group of students and the level of chaos vis-à-vis course registration, I try to spend a significant part of the first class or two getting started on the work of the course. As a way to help students generate background knowledge (page 4) on the reading they are about to do, I ask them to write for 10 minutes or so on the subject "What True Education Should Do." Then we discuss the various philosophies of education that emerge from the student writing. Next I read aloud Sydney J. Harris's essay, "What True Education Should Do" (page 5). I ask students to work in pairs to use clues to guess at the meaning of an unfamiliar word (page 6). Then I ask them to use one or more strategies for responding to the reading: annotating (page 7), clustering ideas (page 8), making double-entry notes (page 9), or taking notes (page 10). Additionally or alternatively, I ask them to make a journal entry on the reading (page 11).

During this time, I move around the room, stopping to answer questions and make suggestions. For example, I remind some students not to write long summaries when they make double-entry notes. If individual students seem to have writer's block when it comes to the journal entry, I briefly discuss with them their reactions to the reading and encourage them to record those reactions without focusing on the mechanics of writing.

I then ask students to share their reactions to the reading. I prefer to have students talk about what they wrote rather than read exactly what they wrote. I try to have every student make a contribution, which means that I limit my own talking. When things go well, I can walk around the room nodding to students to indicate their turn and let the students' voices dominate the class. After a few or all of the students have spoken, I encourage them to interact with one another, for example, by pointing out that they have different interpretations of the reading and asking them to discuss why that is so.

For the next class, I assign another brief reading selection, for example, "Barriers" (pages 13–15) or "Waiting in Line at the Drugstore" (pages 16–19), along with the Write After You Read activity that follows the reading. When students come to the next class, they take turns sharing what they have written. If there are new students, I ask for a student volunteer to summarize the reading so that the new students can feel included in the class and can follow and contribute to the subsequent discussion.

READINGS

In addition to the argumentative essay, "What True Education Should Do" by Sydney J. Harris, Chapter 1 includes two essays based on the writers' experiences: "Barriers" by Rolando Niella and "Waiting in Line at the Drugstore" by James Thomas Jackson. Together, these readings set the stage for several of the major themes that emerge in the readings in Part Two of *Guidelines*: learning, language, communication, literacy, and migration.

Reading 1 (pages 13–15)

Barriers   *Rolando Niella*

In this essay, written in his first year of college, Rolando Niella compares the experience of learning a second language to the experience of learning how to play tennis. He reveals the frustration and discouragement that occurs when he cannot sustain a conversation or keep a ball in play. Yet he concludes that practice will result in mastery and that the effort is worthwhile.

For this student essay, I use discussion activities that are similar to those used for the professional essays. This method gives students a sense of a student writer as a *writer* and helps them recognize that what they themselves write will become reading for someone else. "Barriers" is not presented as a perfect model. Any discussion of how Rolando Niella could have strengthened the essay is worthwhile.

Reading 2 (pages 16–19)

Waiting in Line at the Drugstore   *James Thomas Jackson*

James Thomas Jackson describes how he became a writer after dropping out of school at age 13. Sent by his employer to buy food and supplies, he is forced to wait in line at a drugstore until white people are served first. While waiting, he reads book after book from a bookcase in the store and becomes aware not only of white American writers but also of African-American writers whose existence had been ignored in his schooling.

Two points students may debate in this essay are why Jackson's wait time eventually becomes shorter and why the waitresses come to treat him with "a sense of graciousness" (page 18). Another question worth discussing is the influence of African-American writers on Jackson's own writing career. Would his life have had the same outcome if he had read only non-African-American writers?

I supplement the reading with photographs and documents of the period, such as those in A *Pictorial History of African Americans: Newly Updated Edition* by Langston Hughes et al. (Crown, 2005).

Further Reading:
Acosta, June, ed. *Waiting in Line at the Drugstore and Other Writings of James Thomas Jackson*. Denton, Texas: U of North Texas P, 1993.
Kennedy, Stetson. *Jim Crow Guide: The Way It Was*. Boca Raton: Florida Atlantic UP, 1990.

READINGS AND WRITING ASSIGNMENTS

Part Two includes four chapters of readings and accompanying essay assignments that, together, ask students to write from experience, relate what they read to what they have experienced, analyze an argumentative essay, and analyze a work of fiction. I believe that an essay assignment is most meaningful if it is viewed as a stage in a sequence of tasks so that students know they have multiple opportunities to build on their own learning and thinking. Accordingly, the guidelines that follow each assignment take students through various stages of developing an essay. As students develop their essays, of course, they may find that the stages interact or overlap, and they may add new stages to the process.

While the assignment in Chapter 2 instructs students to write from their own experiences, the assignments in Chapters 3 through 5 instruct students to write about the course readings. These assignments allow students to frame their own questions about the assigned readings. This helps students create a bridge between achieving a satisfactory comprehension and interrogation of another author's ideas and creating an analytical argument of their own. Ideally, through writing, students will gain insight into why authors have shaped their writing in particular ways or will discover previously unnoticed connections between ideas or issues.

Chapter 2
Writing from Experience

Most students can write from sources more easily if they first gain confidence using written language to write from their own experience or background knowledge. This chapter does not focus only on students' own experiences and background knowledge, however. Students are asked to respond to what they read, for example, by writing journal entries or by answering the discussion questions that follow the reading, and can thereby strengthen the critical reading strategies they practiced in Chapter 1.

READINGS

The reading selections in Chapter 2 are based on the writers' experiences with living in multiple worlds. Given the students' familiarity with the subject matter, these readings have produced powerful reactions from students in my own writing classes and have motivated students to write. The readings have the added benefit of providing significant cultural or historical material for us to discuss. I myself enjoy reading these selections again and again, so I find it a pleasure to present them to students. Two of these selections can be categorized as works of fiction. Anzia Yezierska's piece is taken from a novel, and Zitkala-Ša's piece is fictionalized autobiography.

Reading 1 (pages 24–30)
The School Days of an Indian Girl   *Zitkala-Ša*

In this selection, Zitkala-Ša describes the experience of a Native-American child who voluntarily left her reservation at the age of eight to attend an English-only mission school for Native Americans. Unable to speak or understand English and treated rudely, she is frightened and lonely. Within a year, with her English strengthened, she rebels by deliberately misinterpreting an instruction and mashing hated turnips through the bottom of a jar.

The writing may at first appear to be an innocent retelling of a difficult adjustment to school. But a close rereading may reveal that underlying Zitkala-Ša's words are criticism and mockery of European Americans, in particular of the missionaries in the boarding school. Countering the prevailing stereotype that Native Americans are savages, whereas European Americans are civilized, for example, she describes the uncivilized behavior of white women, who use physical violence to discipline children, in contrast to her mother's method of reasoning quietly. Students may debate whether the child's rebellion is a positive or negative outcome of her experience.

I supplement this reading with photographs, such as those from Rayna Green's *Women in American Indian Society* (Chelsea, 1992).

Further Reading:
Spack, Ruth. "Transforming Women: Zitkala-Ša's *American Indian Stories*," in Ruth Spack, *America's Second Tongue: American Indian Education and the Ownership of English, 1860–1900.* Lincoln: U of Nebraska P, 2002. pp. 142–170.
Susag, Dorothea M. "Zitkala-Ša (Gertrude Simmons Bonnin): A Power(full) Literary Voice." *Studies in American Indian Literatures* 5 (Winter 1993): 3–24.

Reading 2 (pages 30–35)
My English   *Julia Alvarez*

In this essay, Julia Alvarez describes how English went from being the language that kept her parents' secrets to the language that opened her up to new ways of self-expression. She explains how she acquired the language and internalized it only after moving from the Dominican Republic to the United States, where her ongoing experience with English led her to relax enough to develop a felt sense of the language and its meanings. Her experience was enhanced by the affirmative pedagogical strategies of her sixth-grade English teacher. Alvarez's story demonstrates how practice, immersion, creativity, encouragement, and support can enable second language learning.

Alvarez's experience in the Dominican Republic strikes many students as unique, for her parents sent her to an English-only school rather than to a bilingual school or to a school whose medium of instruction was Spanish. Nevertheless, they identify with her struggle to learn the new language and with her growing understanding of different ways to use language, including Spanglish. The students in my classes have had fruitful discussions about how Alvarez's sixth-grade teacher instilled a love of writing in her. This classroom scene reappears in *Guidelines* in Activity: Synthesizing two sources (pages 256–258), where students are asked to compare it to a classroom scene from Esmeralda Santiago's *When I Was Puerto Rican*. In the Santiago piece, the English teacher's assignment discourages the student's impulse to write.

Further Reading:
Alvarez, Julia. *Something to Declare: Essays*. Chapel Hill, NC: Algonquin Books, 1998.
Silvio, Sirias. *Julia Alvarez: A Critical Companion*. Westport, CT: Greenwood Press, 2001.

Reading 3 (pages 35–41)
College   *Anzia Yezierska*
In this excerpt from an autobiographical novel, Anzia Yezierska conveys the disappointment of a poverty-stricken immigrant who finds that college life is not what she had hoped for. Impressed by the beauty of the campus and of the students, the narrator wants to become an integral part of this scene. Overworked, rejected, and humiliated by her isolation, she ultimately finds strength in the realization that her suffering pales in comparison to the pain that others have experienced.

Students may identify strongly with the narrator ("This story is so true!") or they may find her too rude or too self-pitying ("I understand that she was poor and wanted her life to change but nothing can change overnight, and she's got to learn to live with that."). They may find the writing powerful ("the sense of loss of the author was digging into the reader's heart"), or they may consider it melodramatic.

I supplement this reading with photographs of the Lower East Side in New York City at the turn of the twentieth century. Jacob Riis's *How the Other Half Lives: Studies Among the Tenements of New York* (New York: Scribner's, 1890) is a good resource. It can be found online at www.cis.yale.edu/amstud/inforev/riis/title.html.

Further Reading:
Harris, Alice Kessler. Introduction. *Bread Givers*. By Anzia Yezierska. New York: Doubleday, 1975. v–xviii.
Henriksen, Louise Levitas. *Anzia Yezierska: A Writer's Life*. New Brunswick: Rutgers UP, 1988.

Reading 4 (pages 42–46)
A Book-Writing Venture   *Kim Yong Ik*
Kim Yong Ik writes of how he decided to become a writer in English during the time he was a college student in the United States, even though he struggled with the language. He explains how the differences between English and his first language, Korean, created stumbling blocks along the way, how he read

literature in English as he consistently worked on his craft, and how he ultimately succeeded in publishing his work. His story demonstrates not only the importance of practice, persistence, and belief in one's self but also the significant role that reading can play in developing writing ability.

This inspirational story rarely fails to impress students with their own potential and possibilities in the English language. It also creates a lot of discussion about the difficulty of translation, given the differences between languages and cultures, with students providing examples from their respective backgrounds.

Further Reading:
Cheung, King-Kok. *An Interethnic Companion to Asian American Literature.* NY: Cambridge UP, 1996.
Kim, Yong Ik. *The Happy Days.* Boston: Little, Brown, 1960.

Reading 5 (pages 46–51)
Mother Tongue   *Amy Tan*

Amy Tan explains how she uses different versions of English for different occasions, for example, a standard English that she learned at school and a family English that she uses with her mother, whose first language is Chinese. Tan says that, although her mother's reading ability is sophisticated, her spoken language is often characterized by others as deficient. Nevertheless, Tan sees strength in its images, creativity, and rhythm. Tan indicates that her own language development was shaped by her familial experience, causing her teachers to try to steer her away from writing to more quantitative studies, but her rebellious nature pushed her to pursue her interests. She found success as a writer when she envisioned her mother as the reader of her stories and embraced all of the Englishes she knew.

Students respond well to this essay, and my classes have had many rich discussions about the varieties of languages they know and how language has shaped their own identities and career paths. One of the most poignant responses I have read in a journal entry came from a student who gained a new appreciation of her own mother's spoken language after reading "Mother Tongue":

> Amy Tan's passage hit very close to home. The experiences she shared with her mother and the English her mother speaks are similar in nature to some of the experiences my mother and I have shared. . . . [T]he English my mother speaks sometimes does embarrass me and even nowadays I still wish that she was able to speak what I deem to be "proper" English. However, in reading this article I have realized that it is true that who is to say what is "proper" English. I can understand the English my mother speaks perfectly and she understands the English I speak. So who is to say that we are not able to communicate as effectively as anyone else?

Further Reading:
Huntley, E. D. *Amy Tan: A Critical Companion.* Westport, CT: Greenwood, 1998.
Snodgrass, Mary Ellen. *Amy Tan: A Literary Companion.* Jefferson, N.C: McFarland, 2004.

GUIDELINES

In this section of Chapter 2, students are able to see the process undertaken by a student named Rolando Niella as he applied the recommended guidelines to produce his own essay, "Barriers," which appears in Chapter 1 on pages 13–15. This is an eye-opener for many students. Earlier journal entries, written just after they had read the completed essay, reveal some students' insecurity about writing: "I wish my pepers will be as good as the 'Barriers' but I don't think they will be. I can't think of a topic orginal enough and within my knowledge." As they later watch the unfolding of his essay, however, their reactions change: "I was very impressed by the way his essay improved. I could tell that he put a lot of time and effort to the essay. Now I understand that I can do it too."

Although I mention in class several times that Rolando's writing was corrected for publication, many students believe he was able to write without making errors. To disabuse them of this idea, I show students this sample of his actual writing (which was originally a handwritten mess!):

> *Are they bodered by my language problem, can't they carrie on coversation with me because they always talk about local or national subject of which I 'not inform. This is really hard and some time make me feel like an estranger in a group were everybody is lauphin and talking and they sopposly were my friends.*

Essay Assignment (page 52)

One of the traps of an essay based on experience can be merely to recount events rather than to find insight or meaning in the experience. I find that when, under my guidance, students have the opportunity to share their experiences in class and ask each other questions for the purpose of uncovering meaning, the resulting essay is more satisfactory.

Note: Although I typically begin my course with the readings in this chapter, I don't necessarily use them to lead to an essay that focuses on writing from experience. I sometimes assign the essay assignment in Chapter 3, Relating Reading to Experience. If I have a particularly advanced group of students, I might assign students to synthesize the readings to develop generalizations or theories about such themes as living in multiple worlds or communicating across languages and cultures. Or I might ask them to read LaRay M. Barna's "Intercultural Communication Stumbling Blocks" in Chapter 3 (pages 66–74) and apply it to one or more of the readings in Chapter 2. For any of these assignments, I find the *Guidelines for Synthesizing* in A Handbook for Writing to be useful (page 255).

Exploring a Topic (pages 52–61)

In class, students practice several brainstorming strategies to get started on and develop ideas for an essay. I spread these writing activities out over time. Teaching these strategies can be fun, but the techniques don't work for everyone. Some students may find them useless at first but then, with more practice, use them successfully. As long as I present them as strategies and not as rules that must be followed, the techniques can enhance the classroom experience. I usually write along with students and we share what we have written.

Making a List (pages 52–53)

Students can work alone or in groups to generate lists. Some of the topics they come up with may sound outrageous, but I encourage them to take risks to enliven the assignment. This activity can be completed in 10 minutes or less.

Freewriting (pages 53–54)

I usually give students approximately 10 minutes to write individually, with instructions to keep the pen moving and to write "I have nothing to say" over and over until an idea emerges. Most students seem to find this to be a liberating experience, but some may be intimidated at first; so I am always prepared to offer aid to anyone who seems paralyzed by the task by carrying on a private conversation that helps the student to brainstorm ideas.

Looping (pages 54–56)

This activity is an extension of the freewriting exercise, but looping also asks students to reflect on what they have written. I often stop after each loop and ask some students to read aloud what they have written or to read just the summary sentence. I sometimes volunteer to read my own "loop" first to get things going. Sometimes this activity goes quickly; sometimes it takes a long time. If we run out of time, students can finish looping outside of class.

Cubing (pages 57–60)

The secret of successful cubing is to spend only 2–3 minutes on each perspective. The fast pace stimulates the imagination. I often stop after one or two perspectives to see what students have written, to get their reactions, and to encourage them to go on. This activity can take a long time and can be completed out of class. I have sometimes brought to class Tootsie Roll Pops or other objects to encourage students to stretch their imaginations to generate ideas. The lollipop tends to tap into childhood memories, which can lead some students to a topic for the first essay.

Clustering Ideas for Writing (pages 60–61)

Clustering can be an especially effective visual technique. Clustering also appears as a reading strategy in Chapter 1 (page 8) as a way to create a map of the ideas in a reading selection.

▨ Focusing Ideas (page 61)

After they have explored a topic, it is a good idea for students to start thinking about how to make sense of all they have written up to this point. I do not think of focusing as writing a thesis. The term *thesis* may be useful for some students but, in my experience, it is paralyzing for many others, especially at this early stage. When I talk to students about their writing, I often ask, "What do you think you want to focus on?" or "What are you focusing on?" These types of questions seem to have more real-life qualities than "What is your thesis?" and thus are relatively easy for students to answer informally in a way to help them shape their ideas. Students will be directed back to this guidelines box when they are composing the essay assignments that appear later in the book.

Structuring the Essay (pages 62–63)

To organize essays based on experience, whose structure is determined largely by the writer's subject matter and intention, the best advice, I believe, is simply to have an overall framework: beginning, middle, and ending. My own reading of hundreds of published personal essays suggests that few have a "thesis" in the first paragraph, and so – still avoiding the word *thesis* – I offer make-a-point-at-the-beginning as only one option among others. For some students, the organizational pattern is clear from the outset; they may make mental or written outlines. For others, the pattern does not emerge until after they have written one or more drafts. Often my feedback on drafts relates to revising for a more logical organization. The flow chart on pages 62–63 shows three different possibilities for structuring an essay based on experience.

Writing the Essay (pages 63–64)

This paragraph directs students to consult Section II of A Handbook for Writing, where they can receive guidance in drafting, exchanging feedback, and revising their essays. Included here, too, is a checklist titled *Evaluative Criteria for Writing an Essay from Experience* (page 64), which students can apply to their own drafts, to their classmates' drafts, or to the sample student essay by Rolando Niella, "Barriers" (pages 13–15).

Completing the Essay (page 64)

This paragraph reminds students to proofread, edit, and prepare clear final copies of their essays. It also directs them to the relevant pages in A Handbook for Writing for specific guidance.

· ·

Chapter 3
Relating Reading to Experience

Chapter 3 builds on what students have accomplished in Chapter 2. By writing from their own experience, students have practiced exploratory writing and have used details and examples to clarify points. They will now learn how to integrate material from their experiences with material from the reading. Chapter 3 should be used concurrently with A Handbook for Writing, especially to guide students through the processes of citing, summarizing, paraphrasing, and quoting sources.

READINGS

The reading selections in Chapter 3, three of which are research studies, lend themselves well to the essay assignment, which asks students to determine the truth, or validity, of an author's ideas by testing them against their own experiences. The issues addressed in the readings – communicating, learning, and reading – are part of students' common experiences.

Reading 1 (pages 66–74)
Intercultural Communication Stumbling Blocks   *LaRay M. Barna*

Barna examines five barriers to successful cross-cultural communication: language, nonverbal signs, preconceptions and stereotypes, the tendency to evaluate, and high anxiety. She believes that awareness of these stumbling blocks, knowledge of the values and attitudes of other cultures, and a nonjudgmental attitude can help to facilitate communication.

Most students can match their own experiences to Barna's categories. As students compare their own experiences with Barna's findings, however, they may critically evaluate her work. They may find, for example, that she herself perpetuates stereotypes, that her solutions are simplistic, or that she puts too much pressure on international students to do the work of successful intercultural communication.

The professional jargon can make this selection difficult to read. Some students may initially struggle to understand it, but they usually find the article accessible because of the inclusion of student quotations.

Further Reading:
Garrod, Andrew. *Crossing Customs: International Students Write on U.S. College Life and Culture.* New York: RoutledgeFalmer, 1999.

Reading 2 (pages 75–82)
Social Time: The Heartbeat of Culture   *Robert Levine, with Ellen Wolff*

Levine and Wolff's research reveals that ideas of time, punctuality, and pace of life are closely bound to culture and differ from place to place. These differences, when not understood, lead to confusion when people from different cultures interact. Though speed is often equated with progress in industrialized countries, such as the United States, the authors warn that a fast pace of life may compromise health and may therefore be undesirable.

Because Levine begins the essay by describing with humor his own experience as a North American professor in Brazil, this research report is accessible and amusing to most students. As students compare their own experiences with Levine's findings, they may critically analyze his work, however. They may find, for example, that he is guilty of some of the very stereotyping he objects to.

Further Reading:

Levine, Robert V. *A Geography of Time: The Temporal Misadventures of a Social Psychologist, or How Every Culture Keeps Time Just a Little Bit Differently.* New York: Basic, 1997.

Reading 3 (pages 82–90)
Creativity in the Classroom   *Ernest L. Boyer*

Boyer finds that the lecture mode of teaching prevails in college classrooms, sometimes characterized by bored professors and disinterested students. He argues that universities should give priority to basic undergraduate courses: The finest teachers should teach first-year students, and classes should be small to allow for interaction and collaborative activities and thus active student engagement. Effective teaching means that the instructor has good command of the subject and is optimistic, involved, and sensitive.

Lively discussion often ensues as students compare their own classroom experiences to Boyer's findings. They may critically analyze his work, for example, by disagreeing with some of his conclusions about gender issues or about effective teaching.

Further Reading:

Boyer, Ernest L. *College: The Undergraduate Experience in America.* New York: Harper, 1987.

Burgan, Mary. "In Defense of Lecturing." *Change* 38.6 (2006): 30–35.

Reading 4 (pages 90–95)
The Art of Reading   *Lin Yutang*

Lin Yutang argues in favor of habitual reading, saying that those who do not read have limited lives and perspectives, for reading takes people into multiple worlds. The best reading experiences move the reader beyond the learning of facts into contemplation. The point of reading is not to become an educated person but to cultivate "personal charm" as a thinker and "flavor in speech" as well as in writing (page 91). Rather than reading out of obligation, people should choose books at whatever time, place, and circumstance will be most pleasurable. Over time, upon reflection, and as a result of the interaction between reader and writer, the meaning of books changes. The art of reading, for Lin, entails reading spontaneously and for pleasure, especially the works of a favorite author.

This essay usually creates lively debates, as students support or refute Lin's various points. Some take issue with his point that reading a newspaper is not really reading, for example, or they argue that the purpose of reading is indeed to become educated. Students also talk about their own reading experiences, which they've written about in the Write Before You Read activity, and share their favorite authors.

Many students express the desire to read a book after reading Lin's essay. One of the book reading projects I have assigned is for students to go to a large bookstore, study its contents according to the categories in which books are displayed, and select a book (any genre) for themselves; if they can't afford it, they can borrow it from the library. This often proves to be rewarding, especially for students who have never done this before and who feel changed by the experience of perusing books in this way. Sometimes students bring friends with them to find a book, and they may spend hours together searching. A number of students buy more than one book, for future reading. They write summaries and evaluations of the books they read and share them with the class.

Further Reading:
Furman, Laura, and Elinore Standard, eds. *Bookworms: Great Writers and Readers Celebrate Reading*. New York: Carroll, 1997.
Quindlen, Anna. *How Reading Changed My Life*. New York: Ballantine, 1998.

GUIDELINES

In this section of Chapter 3, students are able to see the process undertaken by a student named Doxis Doxiadis as he applied the recommended guidelines to produce an essay relating LaRay M. Barna's research study, "Intercultural Communication Stumbling Blocks," to his own experience as an international student.

Essay Assignment (page 96)

This essay assignment asks students to examine the relationship between what they have read and what they know from experience. Its purpose is to illuminate, evaluate, or test the validity of the ideas expressed in the reading. I work concurrently with Section I of A Handbook for Writing (pages 236–258) so that students can learn about and practice the processes of citing, summarizing, paraphrasing, quoting, and synthesizing sources.

Exploring a Topic (pages 96–100)

The exploratory strategies described in Chapter 2 (pages 52–61) may be useful for students, but to fulfill this new type of essay assignment, which involves evaluating a reading, students need to develop new strategies that will enable them to incorporate direct references to the text.

Selecting a Reading (pages 96–97)

The first step in writing about a reading is, of course, to select the reading. Looking over their journal entries is typically the best way for students to be reminded about what interests them most. Looking at the questions that follow the readings, too, will spark their memories about the readings.

Taking Notes on a Reading (pages 97–98)

Students will choose the most effective way to take notes, but they should be directed back to the *Guidelines for Taking Notes on the Reading* in Chapter 1 (page 10) for further guidance.

Selecting Experiences That Relate to a Reading (pages 98–100)

Students may find the exploratory strategies from Chapter 1 useful in generating ideas for their essays. As a way to generate more ideas, they can also work in pairs or in small groups to discuss their experiences.

Focusing Ideas (page 100)

The students' focal points at this stage can consist of one or more sentences. It is important that they make clear that there is a relationship between what they have read and what they have experienced, either because their experiences support or refute the findings reported in the reading, or both. Students should be reminded that the focus may change as they begin the actual writing. Students will be directed back to this guidelines box when they are working on later essay assignments in *Guidelines*.

Structuring the Essay (pages 100–108)

For the previous essay assignment, Writing from Experience (pages 62–63), I outline the structure by using the general words *beginning*, *middle*, and *ending*. Here I use the conventional terms of academic writing – introduction, body, conclusion – to reflect the new kind of essay that students are being asked to produce. Students will be directed back to these guidelines boxes when they are composing the essay assignments that appear later in this book. The flow chart on page 101 is specific to an essay that relates reading to experience.

The Introduction (pages 101–104)

The *Guidelines for Writing an Introduction* are generic, designed to be applied to a variety of academic essay assignments. More specific guidelines are included in each chapter for the particular essay assignment. Here, for example, I offer the recommendation to provide "a focal point that reveals your perspective on the relationship between the ideas in the reading and your own experiences" (page 101). Students will be directed back to the generic guidelines box when they are working on later essay assignments in *Guidelines*.

···▸ Activity: *Evaluating introductions* (pages 102–104)

Students can develop a sense of what an effective introduction to an essay that relates reading to experience might look like by analyzing these sample student introductions. In my experience, students react quite differently to each introduction, so there can be no one "right" analysis. It is more useful to examine how fully an introduction engages a reader and fulfills expectations than to determine how successfully it fits a formula. Because readers bring their own backgrounds and values to what they read, answers will vary.

The Body (pages 104–107)

Again, there is no formula for writing body paragraphs, so the *Guidelines for Structuring the Body Paragraphs* (page 105) should be treated as exactly that – generic guidelines. I offer three more specific possibilities for structuring the body paragraphs of an essay relating reading to experience (pages 105–106) as a way to make students aware that this is a flexible process dependent on the reading's content and the writer's intent and that the organizational pattern can be revised over time. Students will be directed back to the generic guidelines box when they are working on later essay assignments in *Guidelines*.

Activity: *Evaluating body paragraphs* (pages 106–107)

Students can develop a sense of what an effective body paragraph might look like in an essay that relates reading to experience by analyzing these sample student paragraphs. Because readers bring their own backgrounds and values to what they read, answers will vary.

The Conclusion (page 108)

Most of us have difficulty writing conclusions, and the best advice I have been able to come up with is that a conclusion grows out of the material presented in the body of the essay. So students may need to reread the middle of their papers in order to see what evidence they have actually provided. They should be reminded, however, that the best conclusions do not merely repeat what has been said but bring readers beyond the material already presented to think more deeply about the issue at hand. Precisely because conclusions grow out of the material already presented, it made no sense for me to include an isolated activity for evaluating conclusions. But I would recommend looking back at the course readings to analyze how different authors conclude their essays. Students will be directed back to this guidelines box when they are working on later essay assignments in *Guidelines*.

Writing the Essay (pages 108–109)

This paragraph directs students to consult Section II of A Handbook for Writing, where they can receive guidance in drafting, exchanging feedback, and revising their essays. Included here, too, is a checklist titled *Evaluative Criteria for an Essay Relating Reading to Experience* (page 109), which students can apply to their own drafts or to their classmates' drafts.

Completing the Essay (page 109)

This paragraph reminds students to proofread, edit, and prepare clear final copies of their essays. It also directs them to the relevant pages in A Handbook for Writing for specific guidance.

Chapter 4
Analyzing an Argumentative Essay

In Chapter 4, students are provided the opportunity to strengthen their skills in citing, summarizing, paraphrasing, and quoting. And they can again draw on their own experiences and perspectives, this time to analyze an argumentative essay to determine the strengths and weaknesses of an author's argument.

READINGS

The authors of the readings in Chapter 4 present their opinions on controversial issues in education: what students should be taught, how they should be taught, and how their learning should be assessed. I chose these readings because they are thought-provoking readings that students react strongly to, and these strong reactions typically motivate students to respond in writing to the authors' ideas. The readings are certainly not meant to represent model arguments; all of the essays have flawed reasoning. But the very flaws in the arguments enable students' own insightful analyses. The topic of education – teaching and learning – relates directly to students' present situation, and so they almost always can provide meaningful counterarguments and examples.

I sometimes ask students to debate the educational issues covered in *Guidelines*. They may debate two sides of one essay's issue, or they may compare two essays with opposing or differing viewpoints (e.g., Ho and Hirsch). Students use class time to work together in teams to scour an essay for evidence. (They may also want to consult Boyer's study of the college classroom on pages 82–89.) Then I or another student acts as moderator as the teams take turns presenting and refuting evidence. Although this approach can be quite successful, it runs the risk of disorienting students who have difficulty arguing for views they do not really hold themselves.

Reading 1 (pages 112–114)
We Should Cherish Our Children's Freedom to Think   *Kie Ho*
Kie Ho argues that although American education does not meet high standards in certain basic skills, it is a superior system because it allows for free experimentation with ideas.

Even students who find Ho's argument flawed may find his words and tone persuasive. E. D. Hirsch's article can provide an effective counterargument to this essay. The sample student essay by Sophia Skoufaki in A Handbook for Writing (pages 283–284) responds to the essay directly, examining some strengths and weaknesses of Ho's argument. Students who choose to write about Ho's essay can also cite Skoufaki.

Further Reading:
Langer, Ellen J. *The Power of Mindful Learning*. New York: Perseus, 1998.

Reading 2 (pages 115–117)
Teach Knowledge, Not "Mental Skills"   *E. D. Hirsch*

Hirsch promotes a grade-by-grade core knowledge curriculum in which the same material is offered to children in the same grade. He claims that this program serves to avoid huge knowledge gaps that occur in programs that focus on skills rather than content.

Students may criticize Hirsch for not explaining his terms well enough, especially what he means by "mental skills." Students may take issue with Hirsch's claim of the superiority of his method, especially if they have had a type of core knowledge education in high school. Others may think it's a good idea. Others may note that Hirsch has a vested interest in the promotion of his idea because of his Core Knowledge Foundation.

Further Reading:
Hirsch, E. D. *The Knowledge Deficit*. Boston: Houghton, 2006.

Reading 3 (pages 117–120)
Grades and Self-Esteem   *Randy Moore*

Moore claims that a major reason for students' academic under-preparedness is the "mission" to raise students' self-esteem. Contending that this mission praises self-expression, making all opinions equal, he claims that it is responsible for lower standards and higher grades. He argues that self-esteem can be earned only by reaching high standards.

This essay often leads to introspection as students consider how important their self-esteem is in the educational process, and this also may lead to a class discussion of my own assessment procedures in our writing course.

Further Reading:
Sykes, Charles J. *Dumbing Down Our Kids: Why American Children Feel Good About Themselves But Can't Read, Write, or Add*. New York: St. Martins, 1996.

Reading 4 (pages 121–125)
Confusing Harder with Better   *Alfie Kohn*

Alfie Kohn argues that the emphasis on raising standards is transforming educational institutions into preparation centers for tests, largely because the standard of measurement is the test score result. Teaching to the test compromises students' learning experiences, he contends, for classrooms are becoming sites for treating students not as thoughtful human beings but as containers into which information must be poured. In Kohn's mind, paradoxically, a high test score thus suggests a lower standard. Kohn advocates a curriculum that actively engages students in meaningful and intellectually challenging work rather than a program that requires them to learn facts that are often irrelevant.

Students may need help getting through Kohn's ideas, but once they understand what he is saying, they can identify with the essay's points. In both the United States and elsewhere, students have much experience being tested, and they have much to say about whether what they learn for these tests is valuable or useless, permanent or temporary.

Further Reading:
Kohn, Alfie. *The Case Against Standardized Testing: Raising the Scores, Ruining the Schools.* Portsmouth, NH: Heinemann, 2000.

Reading 5 (pages 125–127)
The Commencement Speech You'll Never Hear   *Jacob Neusner*
Neusner claims that professors inadequately prepare students for the real world because they reward mediocre work and tolerate rude behavior, and he recommends that students unlearn the lessons of college in order to avoid failure in the outside world.

I have received strong, wide-ranging, and often hilarious reactions to this essay: "He told the honest truth." "I could never be a teacher as I do not have the patience and tolerance like Jacob Neusner." "It surprises me that some of the professors only be nice to students to get rid of them. Somehow, I think some students are deserved to be rid." "All I can tell him is just wait and see your misjudgment. We are going to get somewhere whether you believe it or not." "I really think this man fits into the case of social rejection."

The Brown University *Daily Herald* received over two hundred letters within five days of the publication of this essay. Many students accused Neusner of insanity and incompetence and demanded that he be fired (he almost was).

Further Reading:
Neusner, Jacob. *How to Grade Your Professors.* Boston: Beacon Press, 1984.

GUIDELINES

In this section of Chapter 4, students are able to see the process undertaken by a student named Ida Timothee as she applied the recommended guidelines to produce her own essay analyzing Jacob Neusner's "The Commencement Speech You'll Never Hear." Students can also be directed to Section II of A Handbook for Writing (pages 274–284), where they can learn how a student named Sophia Skoufaki drafted and revised her essay analyzing Kie Ho's "We Should Cherish Our Students' Freedom to Think." Sophia's own completed essay, "Is Creativity Suppressed by Knowledge?" appears on pages 283–284.

Essay Assignment (page 128)

This essay assignment asks students to analyze an argumentative essay and to establish and support a position toward some key ideas or issues raised in the reading. A major goal is for students to question what they are reading and to reexamine their own views. Students can analyze one of the reading selections in Chapter 3 or another argumentative essay you may assign. The assignment also allows room for students to use evidence provided by one writer to refute an argument presented by another writer. I work concurrently with Section I of A Handbook for Writing (pages 236–258) so that students can strengthen their skills in citing, summarizing, paraphrasing, quoting, and synthesizing sources.

One of the most important ways for students to prepare for this assignment is to read and reread so that they are familiar with the text they are responding to. But familiarity doesn't necessarily result in an effective essay. A first draft can sometimes be too much repetition of what an author says rather than analysis and evaluation of those ideas. Or students may argue with the author without first explaining the author's position. In a one-on-one conference, we spend time talking about the reading, as opposed to just the student's writing, to achieve that goal. I also work with students to help them paraphrase and to integrate quotations and to take a stance toward the readings. The conference and revising process can acquaint them with ways to develop their arguments.

Exploring a Topic (pages 128–132)

Students may use some of the exploratory strategies they employed for the first two essay assignments, but they also need to develop ways to do a close analysis of what an author says, how well the author expresses the point, and how fairly the argument is presented.

Selecting a Reading (pages 128–129)

Students should select one reading to focus on, but I encourage students to look at other readings that can provide evidence to refute or support the author's ideas. If the whole class writes essays that incorporate ideas from more than one reading, I spend some class time having students create a paragraph of synthesis, using the *Guidelines for Synthesizing* on page 255 in A Handbook for Writing.

Taking Notes on a Reading (page 129)

I believe that students should take notes in the way they find most productive, but at the same time, I ask them to use the template for outlining at least one argumentative essay (page 129) so that they have experience breaking down a reading in this way. If a reading's argument cannot be logically outlined, that in itself may reveal a weakness.

Evaluating Evidence (page 130)

The *Guidelines for Evaluating Evidence* are phrased in the form of questions that I hope students will internalize. I often use the essay by Sydney J. Harris in Chapter 1, "What True Education Should Do" (page 5), as a practice argumentative essay to which the class as a whole can apply these questions.

Identifying Points of Agreement and Disagreement (page 131)

I think it's useful for students to make lists so that they can develop a visual sense of the points the author is making and where they agree or disagree. I typically use the Harris essay (page 5) for practice, and we put Harris's points on the board.

Determining Reasons for Agreement or Disagreement (pages 131–132)

When students draft their essays, they may merely say that an author makes a strong point or a weak point, without providing substantive reasons to explain why they agree or disagree with the author's points. This exercise reminds them to develop evidence in the form of examples, experiences, or material from their other reading. I typically use the Harris essay (page 5) for practice, as I do for identifying points of agreement and disagreement. We look at the points Harris makes and put on the board the reasons why we might agree or disagree with what he is saying. We then analyze the pattern of responses.

Focusing Ideas (page 133)

This exercise is designed to get students to take a position on the reading. As with any other focal point, this one may be revised in the actual process of writing the paper, but it is important for students to understand the purpose of their essay. They should be reminded that they can take a mixed position or even a questioning stance.

Structuring the Essay (pages 133–138)

It helps students to be reminded that the purpose of structuring an essay that analyzes an argument is to move readers toward an understanding of the argument's strengths and weaknesses. The flow chart on page 134 is specific to such an essay.

The Introduction (pages 134–135)

Students should be directed back to the generic *Guidelines for Writing the Introduction* on page 101. On page 134, I offer additional recommendations for the specific essay assignment in this chapter: to summarize "the gist of the author's argument" and to provide "a focal point that reveals your overall position toward the argument." If students have followed the instructions in the Write After You Read activity following each argumentative essay in Chapter 4, they will have written one-sentence summaries of the readings that capture the gist of the author's arguments. I have some students write these one-sentence summaries on the board, and we discuss how they might revise them to include them in their introductions.

Activity: *Evaluating introductions* (page 134)

Students can develop a sense of what an effective introduction to an essay that analyzes an argument might look like by analyzing these sample student introductions. In my experience, students react quite differently to each introduction, so there can be no one "right" analysis. It is more useful to examine how fully an introduction engages a reader and fulfills expectations than to determine how successfully it fits a formula. Because readers bring their own backgrounds and values to what they read, answers will vary.

The Body (pages 136–138)

Students should be directed to the generic *Guidelines for Structuring Body Paragraphs* on page 105. On page 136, I offer three more specific possibilities for structuring the body paragraphs of an essay that analyzes an argument as a way to make students aware that this is a flexible process dependent on the reading's content and the writer's intent and that the organizational pattern can be revised over time.

Activity: *Evaluating body paragraphs* (pages 136–137)

Students can develop a sense of what an effective body paragraph might look like in an essay that analyzes an argument by analyzing these sample student paragraphs. Because readers bring their own backgrounds and values to what they read, answers will vary.

The Conclusion (page 138)

Students should be directed to the *Guidelines for Writing the Conclusion* on page 108, but again, they should be reminded that the best conclusions do not merely repeat what has been said but bring readers beyond the material already presented to think more deeply about the issue at hand. Precisely because conclusions grow out of the material already presented, it made no sense for me to include an isolated activity for evaluating conclusions. But I would recommend looking back at the readings in Chapter 4 to analyze how the different authors conclude their argumentative essays.

Writing the Essay (pages 138–139)

This paragraph directs students to consult Section II of A Handbook for Writing (pages 274–284), where they can receive guidance in drafting, exchanging feedback, and revising their essays. Included here, too, is a checklist titled *Evaluative Criteria for an Essay Analyzing an Argument* (page 139), which students can apply to their own drafts, to their classmates' drafts, or to the sample student essay by Sophia Skoufaki, "Is Creativity Suppressed by Knowledge?" (pages 283–284).

Completing the Essay (page 139)

This paragraph reminds students to proofread, edit, and prepare clear final copies of their essays. It also directs them to the relevant pages in A Handbook for Writing for specific guidance.

Chapter 5
Analyzing Fiction

Chapter 5 builds on students' ability to analyze texts by asking them to apply analytical strategies to works of fiction, or more specifically, to short stories. The chapter adds to students' repertoire of understanding about how texts operate by teaching structural components such as conflict and resolution and literary elements such as plot, character, setting, point of view, and symbolic imagery.

READINGS

The stories in Chapter 5 are meaningful not only for their literary merit but also for the social history they provide of the United States, especially as it relates to the experiences of slaves, immigrants, and exiles. Together the stories have a multicultural focus, but none of the individual stories is meant to represent a whole culture. Each narrative has global as well as specific cultural meanings, raising issues about choices and challenges that most readers grapple with and attempt to resolve.

I often tie library or Web-based research to class discussions of stories without necessarily having students turn the research into a long writing project. For example, teams of students may present a story to the class, each member of the team having done some outside reading to shed light on the background of the story. As they lead class discussions of the story, they provide this information either directly or in answer to other students' questions. These presentations work especially well if students bring in some visuals or present PowerPoint slides with items such as photographs, maps, documents, and quotations. Sample topics have included the following:

- "The Ingrate" by Paul Laurence Dunbar (pages 142–147): an issue related to slavery in the United States, such as the treatment or education of slaves or the abolitionist movement; or an issue related to the Civil War, such as its causes or the role of African-American soldiers
- "In the Land of the Free" by Sui Sin Far (pages 148–155): an issue related to Chinese immigration (or any other group's immigration) to the United States, for example, immigration laws, discrimination against immigrants, or immigrants' contributions to the United States
- "Tito's Good-bye" by Cristina Garcia (pages 158–161): an issue related to Cuba, for example, life in Cuba before and after the turn to Communism, Cuban exile to the United States, or Operation Pedro Pan; or an issue related to undocumented immigrants from South America

In their journal responses to the stories, students can be encouraged to be creative, for example, by constructing an interior monologue for a character in a particular scene or creating a dialogue between characters or authors either within a story or across stories.

I also use various group activities to promote class discussion of the short stories. In one activity, I ask students to act out scenes from the stories, especially those that include a lot of dialogue, for which the participating "characters" and "narrator" get up in front of the class. They may initially engage in a discussion of a story as they talk among themselves to decide whose line is whose, where characters should stand in relation to one another, and what props they need, based on clues in the text. A "director," "producer," or the "audience" of other class members helps them make these decisions.

In another group activity, I ask students to imagine that their task is to create filmed advertisements or trailers for a movie based on a short story in Chapter 5. Students choose a short story and decide which scene or scenes they would select from the story. Then the students explain why they made this selection and how they might film the scene or scenes.

In yet another group activity, I ask students to assume that they are reporters for a local television station that has assigned them to cover one of the stories and to write a news report describing the incident. I instruct students to include quotations from the story in their news report in the form of "interviews" with the character or characters. The class divides into three groups to write three different reports: One group writes a report for a television program that sensationalizes its stories; one group writes a report for a television program that gives the personal angle of a story; and one group writes a report for a television program that provides straightforward coverage of its stories. Each group plans a way to present the report to the rest of the class (the television audience). After the presentations, the class compares the reports by answering questions such as: Which details of the story are emphasized in each report? Why? Which report most helps you understand the story?

Reading 1 (pages 142–148)
The Ingrate *Paul Laurence Dunbar*
Mr. Leckler tells his slave, Josh (Leckler), that he will teach him how to read and write so that Josh won't get cheated when he is subcontracted to work on neighboring farms. He tells Josh he will be able to buy his freedom eventually with the extra money he will make, but Mr. Leckler secretly plans that that day will never come. Josh escapes to Canada through the Underground Railroad, signing his own pass now that he is literate. After working in Canada as a free man, he joins the army to fight for the Union. Mr. Leckler learns what happened to Josh only when he reads the public roster of Josh's regiment, and he then accuses Josh of being ungrateful.

It's worth looking closely at Mr. Leckler, who presents himself as a good person who takes advice from his good wife and has Josh's interests at heart, but who is actually self-absorbed, selfish, and cruel: He says Josh will be able to buy his freedom but plans to raise the price out of Josh's reach. Furthermore, he is guilty of embezzlement: On page 143 he admits to engaging in "peculations." The fact that Josh escapes rather than waiting to buy his freedom suggests that he has little trust in Mr. Leckler.

In addition to being a terrific story laden with irony, this is a wonderful history lesson, which I – or students who have done research – expand on in class. I like to bring in photographs related to plantation slavery, the Underground Railroad, and the Civil War as well as copies of authentic documents from the period. Two good resources are *Free at Last: A Documentary History of Slavery, Freedom, and the Civil War* by Ira Berlin et al. (New Press, 1992) and the National Archives Web site on African American soldiers in the Civil War: www.archives.gov/education/lessons/blacks-civil-war.

When students question whether this story really could have happened, I tell them that it is based on the experience of Dunbar's father, also a trained plasterer named Joshua, who escaped slavery; that some slaves were taught to read and write; and that some slaves were hired out to do work for others. But I emphasize that relatively kind slave owners such as Mr. Leckler were the exception rather than the rule. At the time Dunbar published this story in 1899, the climate was such that it was almost impossible to publish a work that portrayed the brutal reality of plantation life.

Further Reading:
Blassingame, John W. *The Slave Community: Plantation Life in the Antebellum South.* New York: Oxford UP, 1972.

Hanson, Joyce. *Between Two Fires: Black Soldiers in the Civil War.* New York: Franklin Watts, 1993.

Reading 2 (pages 148–156)
In the Land of the Free   *Sui Sin Far*

Their young son, born in China, is taken from Lae Choo and Hom Hing when he arrives in San Francisco without the proper papers. Months pass, but the child is not returned. A white man comes to the house saying he will help them if they give him $500. Hom Hing says he has already given the man almost all of his money and so Lae Choo offers her jewelry. The man takes it, and several months later they are allowed to retrieve their son. When he sees his mother, the boy hides in the white missionary woman's skirts and tells his mother to go away.

Observing closely how the characters relate to one another reveals much about the hierarchical relationships of the times. Lae Choo defers to her Chinese American husband, who in turn defers to white men. Nevertheless, students may view Lae Choo as independent and courageous when pushed to her limit: she offers her jewelry to get her son back when her husband says he has no more money to contribute to the cause. Far from the stereotypical passive Chinese woman, she can be seen as a person whose attitude is aggressive: "Stop, white man; white man, stop!" (page 154).

Sui Sin Far's work, focusing as it does on the multidimensional humanity of her characters, serves as a counterpoint to the many negative images of the Chinese that had appeared in European American writing up to that time. To supplement the reading, I bring in photos of the period such as those in Shin-shan Henry Tsai's *The Chinese Experience in America* (Indiana University Press, 1986).

Note: The name *Sui Sin Far* translates roughly into English as "the Chinese Lily." The meaning depends on the sequence "Sui Sin Far," and thus the name cannot be separated into "Far, Sui Sin" or even "Far," as academic citation convention might have it.

Further Reading:

Ammons, Elizabeth. "Audacious Words: Sui Sin Far's *Mrs. Spring Fragrance*." *Conflicting Stories: American Women Writers at the Turn into the Twentieth Century*. Elizabeth Ammons. New York: Oxford UP, 1991. 105–120.

Chang, Iris. *The Chinese in America: A Narrative History*. New York: Viking, 2003.

Ling, Amy. "Pioneers and Paradigms: The Eaton Sisters." *Between Worlds: Women Writers of Chinese Ancestry*. Amy Ling. New York: Pergamon, 1990. 21–55.

Reading 3 (pages 156–158)

America   Arthur Schnitzler

A man arrives in the United States on a gray nineteenth-century day and has a flashback to his home country and his former lover, Anna. He remembers how joyfully they had talked about America as their own discovery, not Columbus's, a place to which they would travel together; and he associates the memory with Anna's fragrance. As his mind returns to his present situation, however, he sees not the splendor or sweetness that he and Anna had imagined but rather a coldness and falseness in the new city. He experiences not the humor that he and Anna had shared but the pain of loss. He has lost contact with her, has no way to reach her, and knows nothing about her existence. As he begins to walk, Anna's fragrance seems to waft over him.

This story can be understood largely by its images. Students can make lists on the board of the different sets of images: the positive, sensual images of his lost love ("quiet," "fine," "golden," "sweet," "silly," "intoxicated," "kisses," "laughing," "softly"), the imagined America before his arrival ("sweet," "fragrant"), and the America and self he experiences upon arrival ("gray," "unquiet," "large," "cold," "false," "alone," "lost"). His expectations are dashed by the reality of the city and by his loneliness and regret. At the end, however, when he senses Anna's fragrance, he is in touch with the positive and is poised to experience the new country in a different way. He is sustained by his memories of the past.

Students are always taken with this story, largely because it is not the typical immigrant story but rather treats the experience of immigration as a voyage of the senses. The story may be atypical precisely because Schnitzler never traveled to America. It may well be a screen for fantasy: a particular type of American Dream where the newly discovered continent is connected to the "sweet, white patch of skin behind [the] ear" of a lover (page 156) and with the tantalizing scent of the female body. Students who have themselves migrated can speak to their own sense of loss and gain.

Further Reading:

Berman, Russell A. Introduction. *The Road into the Open* by Arthur Schnitzler. Trans. Roger Byers. U of California P, 1992.

Gay, Peter. *Schnitzler's Century: The Making of Middle-Class Culture 1815–1914.* New York: Norton, 2001.

Reading 4 (pages 158–162)

Tito's Good-bye *Cristina Garcia*

Augustin "Tito" Ureña is a Cuban American lawyer who specializes in helping illegal immigrants. His life flashes before our eyes as he dies of a heart attack in his office in the Little Italy section of Manhattan. We learn of his ex-wife, Haydée, who periodically shows up to wring money from him; of his mistress; of his estranged daughter; of his ill and angry son; of his brothers, whom he hasn't seen in five years; of his sister who wants to save his soul; of his dead mother in a Cuban grave; and of his father left alone in Cuba.

For the Cuban Americans in this story, having migrated to the United States means also dealing with the dilemmas and frustrations of political exile. The story poignantly shows how politics can cause disruption and upheaval in families. Through specific cultural details, Garcia reveals the yearning and sense of loss for a homeland to which the characters cannot return: Tito "remembered with longing the great spits of suckling pigs dripping with fragrant juices back in Cuba" (pages 158–59). Nostalgia creates an idyllic past: "Haydée at sixteen . . . was a magnificent sight" (page 160). The cold, impersonal present – "the sliver of concrete she called a balcony" (page 160) – is contrasted with the glory of the past: "her father's vast plantation" (page 160). A once "healthy" and protected son is now filled with "rancor" (page 161). A daughter who "danced to please him" is now "estranged from him" (page 161). For the younger generation, Cuban cuisine has been replaced by "baroque recipes in *Gourmet* magazine"; the Cuban homestead has been replaced by a "brick Colonial house" (page 160). What Cuban life Tito does maintain is compromised by multiculturalism: "a new Cuban-Chinese cafeteria" (page 158). Yet for all the problems and compromises, immigrants continue to arrive on America's shores, ironically allowing Tito to carve out a life up to the second he dies.

Students should discuss the value of Tito's life, looking not just at how he was a victim of politics but also how his own unethical or uncaring behavior led to his isolated death.

Further Reading:

Pérez Firmat, Gustavo. *Life on the Hyphen: The Cuban-American Way.* Austin: U of Texas P, 1994.

Triay, Victor Andres. *Fleeing Castro: Operation Pedro Pan and the Cuban Children's Program.* UP of Florida, 1999.

Reading 5 (pages 162–168)

Albert and Esene   *Frances Khirallah Noble*

Esene's husband, Albert, has recently died, and while having lunch with her husband's argumentative and critical sisters, Esene has a flashback to the time when Albert had taught her to read and write so that she would be more like the women in her adopted country, the United States. Albert insisted that the lessons be kept secret from the rest of the family until Christmas, when Esene would send handwritten cards for the first time.

Esene initially resists the pressure Albert exerts on her to learn. Over time, however, she experiences the power of words and inadvertently reveals the secret, thereby angering her husband's family, who are shocked at the idea that a woman would know how to read. Albert is angry that she revealed the secret before he wanted her to, but he eventually encourages her independent learning and thinking.

Students typically find this story touching and engage in fruitful discussions about the value of reading, writing, and learning, as well as about family and gender relationships. Some students find irony in the story when they perceive Albert as too domineering and controlling, initially leaving Esene little space for her own desires and pursuits, and wanting the lessons only for the Christmas cards. But they admire how he himself grows as he accepts Esene's own growth as a learner and thinker.

Further Reading:

Orfalea, Gregory. *The Arab Americans: A History*. Northampton, MA: Olive Branch Press, 2006.

Shakir, Evelyn. *Bint Arab: Arab and Arab American Women in the United States*. Westport, CT: Praeger, 1997.

GUIDELINES

In this section of Chapter 5, students are able to see the process undertaken by a student named Shinya Nagase as he applied the recommended guidelines to produce his own essay analyzing Cristina Garcia's short story, "Tito's Good-bye."

Essay Assignment (page 169)

The suggested essay assignment asks for a fairly traditional literary analysis. I also invite students to write creatively in response to the stories but remind them to keep in mind the need to analyze and interpret what they have read. For example, students might write a letter to the author or to a character in the story. They might write a letter from one character to an author, or vice versa, or from one character to another. They might write a letter from a character to someone outside the story, for example, the author, a friend, or a character in another story. They could also write the essay in the form of a psychiatrist's case study of a patient (character) or a court scene in which lawyers debate an issue raised in one or more stories. This creative approach can help students overcome the writer's block they may experience when faced with the task of interpreting fiction.

Exploring a Topic (pages 169–173)

The exploratory strategies described in Chapters 2, 3, and 4 may be useful for students, but students will need to develop new ways to approach the process of analyzing a work of fiction.

Selecting a Reading (page 169)

Students may want to select more than one reading, as the assignment suggests, in order to make comparisons between characters or themes from different stories. The fictionalized works of Zitkala-Ša and Anzia Yezierska in Chapter 2 also lend themselves well to comparison.

Examining Elements of Fiction (page 170)

Here students are asked to examine closely the plot, characters, setting, point of view, imagery, and symbolism of a story. I introduce these elements as we are discussing individual stories so that by the time students start writing their essays, the *Guidelines for Examining Elements of Fiction* are a review. Actually, I begin teaching these elements even before I assign the short stories, for example, by assigning in-class writing in which students describe a familiar place and then analyze it: "Describe a familiar room such as the kitchen or your bedroom in your home. Include as many concrete details as you can recall. Then analyze the details you have just described to reveal what they may reflect about you, your family, or the community in which you live." This activity reminds students that they know a great deal about how to create abstractions from concrete details and that they should feel confident applying this skill to their literary reading.

Discovering a Theme (pages 171–172)

Discovering a theme in fiction is quite different from determining the main point of a nonfiction essay, for fiction writers rarely state a theme directly but rather leave it to readers to infer meaning from a story's details. I usually teach students the difference between the moral of a story and a theme by reading one of Aesop's fables (such as "The Ant and the Grasshopper" on page 30). We look at the fable with a moral attached at the end. We can see in this version that there is a clear message: The author is telling people (in the guise of animals) how to behave. And then we consider the fable when the moral statement is removed. Now, seeing that the author is not telling us *how to behave* but is just showing *how people do behave*, we can consider multiple interpretations of the story. The class discussion then focuses on examining the characters' behavior and motivation in order to determine why human beings are the way they are or why things happen as they do.

The Ant and the Grasshopper

In a field one summer's day a Grasshopper was hopping about, chirping and singing to its heart's content. An Ant passed by, bearing along with great toil an ear of corn he was taking to the nest.

"Why not come and chat with me," said the Grasshopper, "instead of toiling and moiling in that way?"

"I am helping to lay up food for the winter," said the Ant, "and recommend you to do the same."

"Why bother about winter?" said the Grasshopper; "we have got plenty of food at present." But the Ant went on its way and continued its toil. When the winter came, the Grasshopper had no food and found itself dying of hunger, while it saw the ants distributing corn and grain every day from the stores they had collected in the summer. Then the Grasshopper knew:

It is best to prepare for the days of necessity.

Selecting Relevant Evidence (pages 172–173)

Once students have discovered a theme in a story, they need to select the evidence they will include in their essays to support the points they want to make about the story. Some students may have difficulty grasping the concept of interpretation, of "reading between the lines," thinking that that concept gives them license to create evidence that is not in the text. So it's important to demonstrate how bringing together different details from a story can support an interpretation. The *Guidelines for Selecting Relevant Evidence* on page 173 offer different suggestions, but for some students, the most useful one is to make lists of details, as in the example of the student writer at work on page 173.

Focusing Ideas (page 173)

Searching for a recurring theme or repeated pattern that will become the focal point of their essays is usually a fruitful process for students. Alternatively, students can develop a focal point by answering this question: "What do you think the author thinks, believes, or envisions?" It might be useful at this stage to differentiate between *analysis*, which involves the process of breaking a story down into its elements to examine those elements closely, and *interpretation*, which involves the process of piecing the elements together to discover a pattern that reveals the story's possible meaning or significance.

Structuring the Essay (pages 174–179)

Students may need to be reminded that the purpose of an essay that analyzes a work of fiction is to move readers toward an interpretation of the story being analyzed.

The Introduction (pages 174–175)

Students should be directed back to the generic *Guidelines for Writing the Introduction* on page 101. On page 174, I offer an additional recommendation for the specific essay assignment in this chapter: to provide "a focal point that reveals a recurring theme."

···▶ **Activity:** *Evaluating introductions* (pages 174–175)

Students can develop a sense of what an effective introduction to an essay that analyzes fiction might look like by analyzing these sample student introductions. In my experience, students react quite differently to each introduction, so there can be no one "right" analysis. It is more useful to examine how fully an introduction engages a reader and fulfills expectations than to determine how successfully it fits a formula. Because readers bring their own backgrounds and values to what they read, answers will vary.

The Body (pages 176–178)

Students should be directed back to the generic *Guidelines for Structuring the Body Paragraphs* on page 105. I offer three more specific possibilities for structuring the body paragraphs of an essay analyzing fiction on page 176 as a way to make students aware that this is a flexible process dependent on the reading's content and the writer's intent and that the organizational pattern can be revised over time.

···▶ **Activity:** *Evaluating body paragraphs* (pages 177–178)

Students can develop a sense of what an effective body paragraph might look like in an essay that analyzes fiction by analyzing these sample student paragraphs. Because readers bring their own backgrounds and values to what they read, answers will vary.

The Conclusion (pages (178–179)

Students should be directed back to the *Guidelines for Writing the Conclusion* on page 108, but again, they should be reminded that the best conclusions do not merely repeat what has been said but bring readers beyond the material already presented to think more deeply about the story. Students should aim to explain what they believe to be the story's larger meaning.

▨ Writing the Essay (page 179)

This paragraph directs students to consult Section II of A Handbook for Writing (pages 274–284), where they can receive guidance in drafting, exchanging feedback, and revising their essays. Included here, too, is a checklist titled *Evaluative Criteria for an Essay Analyzing Fiction* (page 179), which students can apply to their own drafts or to their classmates' drafts.

▨ Completing the Essay (page 179)

This paragraph reminds students to proofread, edit, and prepare clear final copies of their essays. It also directs them to the relevant pages in A Handbook for Writing for specific guidance.

RESEARCH AND WRITING ASSIGNMENTS

Part Three brings together three types of investigations: field research in Chapter 6 and library research and Web-based research in Chapter 7.

Chapter 6

Writing from Field Research

What I like most about a field research project is that students can come to understand how knowledge is constructed, which, I believe, can enhance their reading strategies. When they read research studies after they have done their own field research, they can take a more critical perspective than if they had not been researchers themselves. Knowing how data are generated, organized, and interpreted (and, dare I say, manipulated) gives students insight into academic ways of knowing. In preparation for their own research projects, students can read and analyze the three field research studies in Chapter 3 – "Intercultural Communication Stumbling Blocks" (pages 66–74), "Social Time: The Heartbeat of Culture" (pages 75–82), and "Creativity in the Classroom" (pages 82–90) – in preparation for their own field research projects to see how different methodologies are described and how different authors integrate their own data with others' ideas and observations.

The field research project can be time consuming, especially if students conduct surveys. Students may need a lot of time to accomplish the tasks, and I sometimes need to be involved actively in a number of projects in order to keep them going: helping students set up interviews, distribute questionnaires, and so on. At various points during the six or more weeks that they work on their projects, students make brief oral presentations in teams or to the whole class so that everyone can learn about various methods, processes, successes, and frustrations. I also set aside a class for data analysis.

GUIDELINES

In this section of Chapter 6, students are able to see the process undertaken by a student named Ayse Yeyinmen as she applied the recommended guidelines to produce her own field research essay, "The Relationship Between International Students and U.S.-Born Students: Two Perspectives," which appears on pages 199–203.

Essay Assignment (page 184)

The essay assignment is written in such a way as to provide flexibility for both instructor and students. Students can all be doing the same kind of field research – for example, all conducting interviews or all conducting surveys – or they can be doing different individual projects. What I assign and how I assign it depends upon the class and my goals for the semester.

▓ Selecting a Field Research Topic (pages 184–185)

This assignment can be tied to subject matter that the readings in *Guidelines* address, or instructors can assign other topics or let students choose their own.

▓ Gathering Background Information (page 185)

It can be useful to have students bring to class the documents they have gathered so that the whole class can see a variety of sample artifacts of field research.

▓ Observing (page 186)

I have the whole class practice a brief observation outside of class, one that lasts approximately 10–15 minutes, and we discuss their findings in class. I usually give students options, such as one of the following:

- Students sit in the school cafeteria and observe where other students choose to sit and how they interact with one another. If international students are observed, this assignment can be linked to LaRay M. Barna's research study, "Intercultural Communication Stumbling Blocks" (pages 66–74).
- Students arrive early to one of their own classes and observe what time the instructor and other students arrive and how they each behave at the moment of arrival. This assignment can be linked to Robert Levine's research study, "Social Time: The Heartbeat of Culture" (pages 75–82).
- Students observe one of their own classrooms to analyze the instructor's teaching style by answering questions such as: Does the instructor lecture? ask questions? lead discussions? interact with students? sit? stand? move around? Additionally or alternatively, students can observe the classroom behavior of their classmates. This assignment can be linked to Ernest Boyer's research study, "Creativity in the Classroom" (pages 82–90).

Whichever practice observation students choose to do, they record their observations in detail and interpret their findings according to the *Guidelines for Observing* on page 186.

▓ Interviewing (page 187)

Interviewing can be the central project, or students can conduct an interview for the purpose of gathering information for another project, such as a survey. I sometimes hand out ideas for central projects.

One suggestion is for students to conduct a series of interviews in which they explore several individuals' experiences learning an additional language, using questions that get at the process through which the interviewees succeeded or failed to acquire the language. Students can then compare their findings with the ideas of one or more of the writers in Chapters 2 and 3. Another suggestion is for students to interview a number of other students about their experiences in their writing classrooms, using questions that get at the process through which their interviewees are learning to write, for example: What kinds of work are you being asked to do? What seems to be helping you to develop your writing? What do you find least productive? Student researchers can then look for patterns across these individuals' experiences for the purpose of developing a generalization about the process of learning to write.

Conducting a Survey (pages 187–190)

The students in my class practice this process first by creating a survey questionnaire together and trying it out on each other. They then work in small groups to look for a pattern in their responses. We put the results on the board and play with the numbers to create percentages and to come to some conclusion about what we have found. Before or after this task, we also analyze the sample questionnaires on pages 189–190 by examining the categories that Ayse created in the left margins and determining what the two sets of categories have in common and where they differ.

Focusing Ideas (page 191)

This exercise works best if students frame the focal point as a question that their research project will answer.

Structuring the Essay (pages 191–197)

Following up on the exercise to focus their ideas, students can be reminded that readers of field research reports want to know the answer to the research question. The flow chart on page 192 shows one common four-part structure for a field research essay.

Introduction (pages 192–194)

Students should be directed back to the generic *Guidelines for Writing the Introduction* on page 101. On page 192, I offer additional recommendations for the specific essay assignment in this chapter: to explain "the significance of the issue that has been investigated" and to provide "a focal point that states or implies the questions that the research project is designed to answer."

▸ Activity: *Evaluating introductions* (pages 192–194).

Students can develop a sense of what an effective introduction to a field research essay might look like by analyzing these sample student introductions. In my experience, students react quite differently to each introduction, so there can be no one "right" analysis. It's more useful to examine how fully an introduction engages a reader and fulfills expectations than to determine how successfully it fits a formula. Because readers bring their own backgrounds and values to what they read, answers will vary.

Methods (page 194)

The *Guidelines for Describing Methods* ask students to do something they have not been asked to do for other essay assignments: Describe in some detail the process they went through to develop the essay. Note that in the sample student essay on pages 199–203, the student writer does not actually use the heading "Methods," but she does describe her methodology. I prefer not to hold students to rigid categories if they can write more fluently without them. On the other hand, using specific headings can help some students organize their work.

Results (pages 195–197)

The results section is the longest part of the essay. The *Guidelines for Presenting Results* ask students to explain the patterns or themes that have emerged from their analyses of the research data and to provide evidence from their research to support that analysis. Note that in the sample student essay on pages 199–203, the student writer does not actually use the heading "Results," but she does explain the patterns and themes that emerged from her data analysis. I prefer not to hold students to rigid categories if they can write more fluently without them. On the other hand, using specific headings can help some students organize their work.

Activity: *Evaluating paragraphs that present results* (pages 195–197)

Students can develop a sense of what an effective paragraph that presents results might look like in a field research essay by analyzing these sample student paragraphs. Because readers bring their own backgrounds and values to what they read, answers will vary.

Discussion (page 197)

The *Guidelines for Writing the Discussion Section* ask students to interpret their research findings by stating a generalization or theory that ties everything together and by making recommendations or raising questions that emerge from the research. Some students' topics do not lead to neat conclusions, however. Sometimes, for example, they undertake projects requiring interviews with people who are not as cooperative as students would like them to be. Their final papers may have to focus on method if not enough data emerges to analyze. And so I want to emphasize that the goal here is not for students to produce a "publishable" research study but rather to discover how research is done and how findings can be reported. Note that in the sample student essay on pages 199–203, the student writer uses the alternative heading "Conclusion" rather than "Discussion."

▓ Writing the Essay (pages 198–203)

This paragraph reminds students to consult Section II of *A Handbook for Writing*, where they can receive guidance in drafting, exchanging feedback, and revising their essays. Included here, too, is a checklist titled *Evaluative Criteria for Writing from Field Research* (page 198), which students can apply to their own drafts, to their classmates' drafts, or to the sample student field research essay by Ayse Yeyinmen, "The Relationship Between International and U.S.-Born Students: Two Perspectives" (pages 199–203).

⋯▶ **Activity:** *Applying evaluative criteria* (pages 198–201)

Because readers bring their own backgrounds and values to what they read, answers will vary.

▓ Completing the Essay (page 203)

This paragraph reminds students to proofread, edit, and prepare clear final copies of their essays. It also directs them to the relevant pages in *A Handbook for Writing* for specific guidance.

· ·

Chapter 7
Writing from Library and Web-Based Research

Various stages of research are presented one step at a time, for clarity. In the course of doing the research, however, students will find that the stages overlap. At each stage, they will have a better understanding of what they have already found and a better idea of what they still need to discover.

GUIDELINES

In this section of Chapter 7, students are able to see the process undertaken by a student named Kristyn Marasca as she applied the recommended guidelines to produce her own library and Web-based research essay, "Get in Line: The Extreme Shortage of ESL Classes," which appears on pages 228–231.

Essay Assignment (page 206)

Students usually produce a research essay of 5–10 pages in length, typewritten, and double-spaced. I require students to reference at least three journal articles and at least one book by a knowledgeable researcher. This requirement assures that students will draw on scholarly sources, not just popular sources. As a result, the content of their essays and their own writing can reach a more sophisticated level. I emphasize that they need to include multiple sources so that they can include different perspectives.

▓ Selecting a Library and Web-Based Research Topic (pages 206–207)

This assignment can be tied to subject matter that the readings in *Guidelines* address, or instructors can assign other topics or let students choose their own.

▓ Writing a Research Proposal (pages 207–208)

Sometimes I assign the proposal as a formal assignment, and other times I assign it as a journal entry in which students can informally tell me what they would like to research. I collect the proposals, make a brief comment (such as a suggestion for how to proceed with the research), and return them to the students.

▓ Conducting Library Research (pages 207–213)

I bring students into the library as a class to make sure they are familiar with its resources and know how to locate relevant and appropriate materials. I introduce them to the reference librarians, one of whom sometimes accompanies us. We walk through the reading room and peruse the current periodicals. We walk through the reference section and peruse those sources. To give them practice in using a database or microfilm, I ask them to find a newspaper published on the day they were born to see what news made the front page, which they are quite interested in learning. Students also practice using indexes and computer files to find books, magazines, and journals.

Library research can be extraordinarily frustrating and time-consuming. I try to make more than one visit to the library with the class so that they can use class time and take advantage of my help and the reference librarians' help to find materials. If students have already found sufficient materials, they use this additional library time to evaluate sources, take notes, or discuss their topics with me.

Determining Subject Headings (page 209)

In the classroom, I ask students to follow the *Guidelines for Determining Subject Headings* to make a list of possible search terms, or descriptors, related to their research topics. I usually begin by taking one student's topic and having the class brainstorm search terms, which I write on the board. Then they help each other do the task on their own respective topics. If there is a computer and screen in the classroom, I can show them how to use the terms to do a search online. Otherwise, I do that with them when we visit the library, either online or in hard copy.

Finding Books in the Library (pages 209–211)

Either in class or in the library, I show students what scholarly books look like and encourage them to look at the table of contents, the preface or introduction, bibliography, and footnotes to get a sense of the kind of material that is covered. I find it best to look through online databases or catalogs with students to help them make intelligent selections, and I literally follow them to the stacks in the library to make sure that they understand how to find books with scholarly content, preferably but not necessarily published by university presses. Once they find relevant books, I remind them to write down the key information necessary for a bibliography.

Finding Journal and Magazine Articles (pages 211–213)

I spend time showing students how to access scholarly journals and how to recognize scholars (as opposed to journalists or popular writers). Using the library's databases, we practice checking off choices that will produce full texts (as opposed to just abstracts) from "peer-reviewed" or "refereed" journals, as they are typically called. It is often difficult for students to make intelligent choices when long lists of possibilities appear. Early in the research process, I actually look over individual students' shoulders to help them make appropriate decisions. Once they find relevant articles, I remind them to write down the key information necessary for a bibliography and encourage them to photocopy the article or to e-mail it to themselves, if that is an option.

Finding Newspaper Articles (page 213)

If students are dealing with current topics, news articles and op-ed columns can be especially valuable. Increasingly, these materials are easy to find on the Internet, and I therefore spend less time showing students how to find news sources in the library than I used to.

Conducting Web-Based Research (pages 214–215)

It is a challenge to keep up with changing technologies. Search engines or Web sites may become obsolete, for example. I have attempted to provide students with general guidelines that can be helpful even if the technology changes.

Evaluating Sources (pages 215–216)

The key to evaluating sources is to figure out which sources are reliable and appropriate for college-level research. If there is a computer in the classroom, I can do searches on a practice topic as the whole class watches on a large screen at the front of the room. If not, we evaluate sources by looking at them in the library, online or in hard copy. Together, we analyze what we see, and I help students recognize when we have located sources that address the research issue under investigation but that are unacceptable because, for example, they are papers written by middle school students or are documents of propaganda. If I question a student's sources, I do the same thing for them individually on my office computer or with hard copies they have brought to my office for a one-on-one conference. The reference librarians also provide lists of appropriate Web sites for students' research projects when students explain their topics. It takes a village to raise students to select appropriate sources and use the new technologies effectively and ethically.

▨ Taking Notes on Research Sources (pages 216–218)

It can be a good idea to check students' notes periodically, especially to see that they are matching notes with sources, using quotation marks for an author's exact wording, and keeping track of page numbers. Some students do not understand how specific the documentation must be.

▨ Writing a Progress Report (pages 218–219)

To write a progress report, students stop what they are doing, summarize what they have found to this point, and assess what they have done. In turn, I provide support and give suggestions for how to proceed. I sometimes ask for more than one progress report from individual students or from the whole class.

▨ Focusing Ideas (page 219)

This exercise is extremely helpful for students after they have gathered what might seem like an overwhelming amount of information. I usually ask them to bring all of their research materials to class so that I can guide them through this process.

▨ Writing a Preliminary Outline (page 220)

I take some class time for students to write preliminary outlines under my guidance. To model the process, I typically take at least one student's topic and make an outline on the board as the student explains it.

▨ Structuring the Essay (pages 220–226)

Given that there is so much material to organize, these guidelines may be helpful before students begin drafting. I use the board to outline some suggestions for structuring the body of an essay, using samples from students' own research.

The Introduction (pages 221–223)

Students should be directed back to the generic *Guidelines for Writing the Introduction* on page 101. On page 221, I offer additional recommendations for the specific essay assignment in this chapter: Explain "the significance of the issue that you have investigated" and provide "a focal point that states your perspective toward the issue, raises a question about the issue, or explains the problem that needs to be solved."

⋯▶ **Activity:** *Evaluating introductions* (pages 221–223)

Students can develop a sense of what an effective introduction to library or Web-based research essay might look like by analyzing these sample student introductions. In my experience, students react quite differently to each introduction, so there can be no one "right" analysis. It is more useful to examine how fully an introduction engages a reader and fulfills expectations than to determine how successfully it fits a formula. Because readers bring their own backgrounds and values to what they read, answers will vary.

The Body (pages 223–226)

Students should be directed back to the generic *Guidelines for Structuring Body Paragraphs* on page 105. On page 223–224, I offer three more specific possibilities for structuring the body paragraphs of an essay based on library and Web-based research as a way to make students aware that this is a flexible process dependent on the reading's content and the writer's intent and that the organizational pattern can be revised over time.

⋯⋯▶ Activity: *Evaluating body paragraphs* (pages 224–226)

Students can develop a sense of what an effective body paragraph might look like in a library or Web-based research essay by analyzing these sample student paragraphs. Because readers bring their own backgrounds and values to what they read, answers will vary.

The Conclusion (page 226)

Students should be directed back to the *Guidelines for Writing the Conclusion* on page 108, but again, they should be reminded that the best conclusions do not merely repeat what has been said but bring readers beyond the material already presented to think more deeply about the research topic.

Presenting an Oral Research Report (pages 226–227)

Students can give oral presentations to the whole class or in groups. In my classes, students photocopy outlines of their presentations or prepare a PowerPoint slide to show on a screen while they talk. One student at a time speaks for five to ten minutes and leaves a few minutes for questions. This presentation occurs between the draft and the completed essay. In cases where presentations are more logically constructed than drafts, I suggest that students restructure the drafts.

Writing the Essay (pages 227–231)

This paragraph directs students to consult Section II of A Handbook for Writing, where they can receive guidance in drafting, exchanging feedback, and revising their essays. Included here, too, is a checklist titled *Evaluative Criteria for Writing from Library and Web-Based Research* (page 227), which students can apply to their own drafts, to their classmates' drafts, or to the sample student essay by Kristyn Marasca, "Get in Line: The Extreme Shortage of ESL Classes" (pages 228–231).

⋯⋯▶ Activity: *Applying evaluative criteria* (pages 228–230)

Because readers bring their own backgrounds and values to what they read, answers will vary.

Completing the Essay (page 231)

This paragraph reminds students to proofread, edit, and prepare clear final copies of their essays. It also directs them to the relevant pages in A Handbook for Writing for specific guidance.

A HANDBOOK FOR WRITING

The handbook provides a convenient resource for both instructors and students. Instructors can assign different sections at different points in the semester. Throughout the semester, students can work back and forth between the handbook and the chapters in *Guidelines* as they work on their various essays.

 SECTION I

CITING, INCORPORATING, AND DOCUMENTING SOURCES

Section I, which can be used concurrently with Chapters 3–7, provides detailed explanations and demonstrations of the processes of citing ideas, summarizing, paraphrasing, quoting, synthesizing, and citing and documenting research sources. Activities in this section are designed to help students practice these academic writing conventions and then to apply them to their own essays.

It may take a long time for students to assimilate these ways of writing if they are unfamiliar with the conventions of academic writing or with the expectations of an academic reading audience. With guided practice over time, as they fulfill different assignments that ask them to write from sources, students will gain the confidence and skills needed to write effectively.

Citing Ideas (pages 236–237)

I particularly like to bring students' attention to the list of verbs used to introduce authors' ideas. Students are likely to refer to this list again and again as they work on their essays. I actually refer to the list for my own writing. Answers to the activity on page 237 will vary.

Summarizing (pages 238–241)

Students can summarize the nonfiction excerpts in the activity on page 240 in pairs or groups; different groupings can do different summaries and then present their summaries to the class, for example, by writing them on the blackboard. For this activity, students should refer back to the list of verbs used to introduce an author's ideas on pages 236–237. Answers to the activities on pages 240 and 241 will vary.

Paraphrasing (pages 241–244)

Students can do the activities on pages 243–244 in pairs or in groups. For the activity on paraphrasing on page 244, they should engage in discussions about what a writer really means and practice using a dictionary and thesaurus, under the instructor's guidance, to find alternative words. Answers to the activities on pages 243–244 will vary.

Paraphrasing can be a difficult task. Some students need extra help. I find it useful to work with such students individually, in conference. I read aloud a passage from an assigned reading; they tell me in their own words what it says; they write down what they have just said; and, if it is acceptable, I say, "That's a paraphrase!"

I repeatedly remind students that paraphrasing involves giving credit to the source.

Quoting (pages 245–254)

Students typically need help to learn why, when, and how to quote. Although there are some conventions, decisions about quoting are often individualistic, depending on a writer's purpose and style – and on the taste of the English teacher-reader-critic. My aim is to help students develop a sense of when and how quoting might be appropriate for their particular essays. Answers to the activities on pages 251–254 will vary.

I repeatedly remind students of the importance of making it clear that the material is being reprinted from another source by using quotation marks when they quote an author's exact words or by blocking off a long quotation. At the beginning of the term, I select sentences from journal entries or essays written for previous classes that contain poorly framed quotations, put them on the board, and have students reshape the sentences.

Through journal writing, students have the opportunity to practice selecting and incorporating quotations over time and in relatively nonjudgmental circumstances. In response to their journal entries and essays, I direct them to the appropriate pages for punctuating quotations (pages 249–250) and even to the particular number that corresponds to their error. For example, for an error involving a quotation within a quotation, I write, "See #3 on page 249."

Synthesizing (pages 255–258)

Throughout *Guidelines*, students are asked to synthesize. Synthesis begins as soon as students write journal entries and compare what they have read to their own experiences. Students may synthesize observations and interviews in a field research essay. They will certainly synthesize the material they gather through library and Web-based research. *Guidelines* is versatile enough so that instructors can assign students to write about themes that emerge from the readings within a chapter or across chapters, for example, the theme of communicating across cultures, an assignment that calls upon students to synthesize the readings. Answers to the activity on pages 256–258 will vary.

Documenting Sources (pages 258–271)

This reference section includes a discussion of when and how to document, using APA and MLA citation and documentation formats. I cover the first few pages in class so that students understand the importance of the convention of citing and documenting sources.

Academic Integrity (pages 272–273)

I see plagiarism as an *intent to deceive* and for that reason, I don't use the word *plagiarism* to describe students' *unintentional* violation of academic rules or conventions for documenting sources. My experience has been that most students do not fully understand the rules and conventions of academic writing. And so when students unintentionally violate a rule or convention, I see it as a teaching moment, an opportunity for students to learn. If I determine that the violation is intentional, that the student has indeed plagiarized, I follow the college policy for reporting incidents of plagiarism. That, too, is a learning opportunity for students.

 SECTION II

DRAFTING, EXCHANGING FEEDBACK, AND REVISING

Section II provides guidelines for students to test their ideas on paper and reshape those ideas in response to comments they receive from other students and myself. Section II ends with a sample student essay by Sophia Skoufaki: "Is Creativity Suppressed by Knowledge?" on pages 283–284.

Drafting (pages 274–275)

Here I describe two kinds of drafts: a trial draft and an interim draft. I may ask individual students to show me another full or partial draft if I think they can benefit from the extra writing.

Trial Drafts (pages 274–275)

For the first essay assignment of the semester, I usually have students bring a trial draft to class (and later an interim draft). The purpose of this trial draft is simply to get them started. Some students bring in a whole essay; others half an essay; others one paragraph; others one line crossed out. I accept everything. Once they have started, they have an idea of what they need to do; and they have practical questions. They may work in small groups, sharing reactions and getting ideas for proceeding. Or they may go around the room, briefly describing their project so that the whole class gets a sense of what everyone is doing. Sometimes students ask if they can change their topic at this point, having heard something that sparks new ideas, which, of course, I approve if I think it will be more productive for the student.

Interim Drafts (page 275)

Students may write poorly organized drafts even when they have been given instructions about creating a logical framework. (This was true even in the days when I used the term *thesis*.) This phenomenon is understandable, given the pressures and constraints of a writing course. Some students have not had the time to devote to the essay; others cannot see the problem. Given the opportunity to bring the draft to class for feedback, students are made aware that composing is an evolving process. Of course, this system may have its drawbacks. Knowing that they have extra chances, some students may not put much effort into an early draft. For that reason, I urge them to bring in the strongest possible draft. I remind them that a weak draft can be improved but the improvement may not result in a high quality piece of writing. In contrast, a draft that demonstrates serious, thoughtful engagement with the task is likely to produce excellent results as a result of the revision process.

Exchanging Feedback (pages 275–277)

Productive exchange of feedback between or among students can be a difficult goal to achieve. My own experience differs from year to year, from class to class, and from assignment to assignment. Some classes settle comfortably into pairs or groups of three or four, and the class hums along as students read and comment on each other's drafts. But other classes are uneven, with one group finishing 20 minutes before another or with an entire group unable to make progress. The instruction to show their work to classmates may initially be met with horror. Many students believe that only an experienced English teacher is capable of making meaningful judgments about writing.

Nevertheless, I believe in the value of peer feedback, which I myself have received for all of my writing, including this book. It can help writers internalize criteria for evaluating written work. Students who do not see problems in their own papers might see them in others', and this may help them understand how a reader might react to what they have written.

But before I ask students to share in this very sensitive task of giving and receiving critical feedback, I devote class time to preparing them for it. My own approach has been (1) to model the peer review process by using a short draft by a student from a previous class (with the writer's name removed and with the writer's permission), and (2) to open up discussion about peer feedback so that students can air their concerns. Students have always responded well to the excerpt from Koberg and Bagnall's book on problem solving, which is reprinted verbatim in *Guidelines*: "How to Criticize Painlessly/How to Accept Criticism" (pages 276–277). These authors recommend that negative criticism be placed within the context of positive reinforcement. Equally important is the advice to resist being defensive and instead to accept any negative comments for further evaluation. Students can choose to ignore suggestions that they don't find valuable or workable.

Students may give oral or written responses to one another's work, depending on which approach the instructor or the students themselves deem more effective or useful.

If I think a peer feedback group can benefit from my help, I join the group. If one student is having a problem working within the group, I work individually with that student. As with all teaching practices, I find that quick thinking and flexibility are valuable assets.

Some groups are more comfortable giving oral feedback, usually focusing on the content (rather than the form) of writing, often asking each other questions and giving each other ideas. Alternatively, writing down their reactions to other students' papers can help reviewers organize their thoughts and give the writers something concrete to deal with. When I ask for written rather than oral feedback, I make enlarged photocopies of the Feedback Form on page 277 and have students fill them out and discuss them. After the feedback session, I ask students to write me a note indicating how they might revise their drafts. This note can be a springboard for discussion when we later meet in a one-on-one conference.

I collect the feedback forms when I collect the drafts. I find the written student comments helpful in my own evaluation of the draft, and I write responses to these comments on the form. The feedback forms become part of the students' writing portfolios.

Revising (pages 278–281)

These guidelines are designed to help students see that revising entails more than just correcting errors. I usually assign this section for students to read after they have received feedback. Before the revision due date, some or all students return for a brief conference to show me what they have done on a subsequent draft before a final draft is completed. Sometimes they just rewrite a particular section, such as the opening paragraphs, and show them to me after class or via e-mail, before they complete the final draft. Students have at least a week to revise their papers. On the day revisions are due, I ask them to write a memo in class about their revision to explain what they have changed or retained, and why, and to hand in the memo with their essay. The memo serves as a guide when I read their revisions.

Preparing a Final Copy (page 282)

I emphasize that a neat presentation can have a positive effect on a reader.

LOCATING ERRORS

The existing research on how best to address error is inconclusive, and so the best we can do is to experiment with ways to help students locate their own errors. Students are well served if instructors consider carefully when and how to address error. Most research on composing processes suggests that writing instructors wait to focus on error until the editing stage of writing. That is, students should draft their papers, then instructors should give feedback on content and organization, and then – once meaning is shaped – should attend to error. This approach initially directs attention to meaning, structure, and style rather than to grammar rules and correctness. An early focus on rules and correctness can do more harm than good if students spend too much time worrying about making errors and too little time thinking about how to develop an idea. When students attend to error at a later stage in writing, grammar can be presented not as a way of memorizing rules but as a way of solving problems as they arise out of real writing situations. Locating (not correcting) grammatical errors in students' drafts while at the same time providing feedback on content does not necessarily overburden the student writer. But, in most situations, focusing on communication and inventiveness before grammatical precision is still good advice for most teachers and students.

Given the sometimes overwhelming number of errors and the limited amount of time available to deal with them, each instructor must set priorities in responding to error. The first priority should be comprehensibility. Because the purpose of using a language is to communicate ideas, asking for clarification is a reasonable response. This request for clarification is appropriate in response to an early draft, especially when students' word choices or garbled syntax result in sentences that simply do not seem to make sense. Students can be asked to explain what they mean and then to write down what they said; or they can be asked to rewrite a sentence in two or three other ways and then to consult with the instructor, a classmate, or a tutor to select the most appropriate version.

Another area of attention can be patterns of error, for example, students' most frequent sentence-level errors, such as errors related to sentence boundaries, agreement, verb tenses (which are marked differently in different languages), or verb forms. Although these kinds of errors may not be easy for students to locate on their own, they are relatively easy for instructors to diagnose. Nevertheless, for the reasons mentioned earlier, it may be counterproductive to attempt to address all of the errors students make. Selecting a few frequently made errors or a few categories of errors is, in most cases, the most sensible approach.

It is important to remember, however, that once certain errors are located for students, the students may need no instruction, for they may know the rule but simply have failed to apply it. Furthermore, bringing attention to error is effective only insofar as it provides clues for self-correction. If instructors make it a practice simply to supply the correct answer, students will not undergo the complex cognitive operation to correct error that makes them more likely to remember how to use correct forms. Still, to monitor their own writing successfully, students need a lot of time to recall grammar rules and to apply them, and they need a relaxed environment in which to do so. Computer grammar programs have the potential to offer students such an environment, given that they allow for self-timed, self-guided editing. However, all of the programs I have reviewed to date provide misleading or confusing information, often leading to the creation of new error.

It is worth remembering that error is natural and inevitable, a sign of language learning at work. And it is important to remember as well that to look only at the errors students make is to ignore those aspects of language that students control. Instead of focusing on what is missing from students' writing, instructors can focus on what it offers: ideas, information, and refreshingly original expressions. Positive comments about students' language use can provide the reinforcement that motivates students to take risks and improve. Comments such as "nicely expressed," "you've created a vivid mental picture with these words," or "I appreciate the way you have made this complex idea understandable" next to an accurately formed, effective, or sophisticated statement can help instill pride and confidence in students who lack faith in their ability to write well in English.

Proofreading (page 285)

The *Guidelines for Proofreading* provide a few suggestions to help students locate their own errors and reminds them to check to see that they have followed certain conventions for writing about sources. Answers to the activity on page 285 will, of course, vary.

Causes of Error (pages 286–288)

Through a trial-and-error process and by hypothesis testing, second language learners progress through various, somewhat predictable stages as they slowly achieve closer and closer approximations of the target language. Students should not be viewed as producers of flawed or deficient language but rather as intelligent, resourceful individuals who are progressing through systematic stages of acquisition. In fact, when students analyze the causes of their own errors, they often reveal a complex thinking process underlying the problem and can come to understand the logic and even inventiveness of what they have produced. While this process does not necessarily result in immediate elimination of that error, it can heighten students' awareness and allow for a positive rather than a negative evaluation of what they have done. This approach may help ease the stress that writing for academic purposes can incur. Furthermore, when instructors show understanding of this phenomenon, it can help students build confidence and take risks.

Students will discover causes of error other than those listed in *Guidelines*. The suggestion to keep a record of the causes of their errors is followed by students who find it useful. Answers to the activity on page 288 will, of course, vary.

Editing (page 288)

The *Guidelines for Editing* remind students to attempt to locate their errors, to analyze the cause of those errors, and to turn to Section IV of A Handbook for Writing for guidance on correcting errors. Answers to the activity on page 288 will, of course, vary.

 **SECTION IV**

CORRECTING ERRORS

I bring the attention of the whole class to these pages, but I rarely use them to teach grammar to the whole class. Rather, I refer to these pages when I help individual students work on issues that arise out of their own writing.

When I locate error for students, I typically just underline an error and ask students to correct their own work and to consult with me or someone else for those errors that they cannot correct on their own. If I leave class time for this process, I move around the room to help individual students with problem areas. If they do not know how to make a correction, I might explain something on the spot or show where the student can find help in this handbook or in another resource. Many of these issues are resolved by discussing what students mean rather than what grammar rule they missed, however (e.g, "Which event happened first, and how can you make that clear?" rather than "You should have used the past perfect tense here"). I ask for clarification if students' word choices or garbled syntax result in sentences that simply do not seem to make sense. Usually, I ask students to explain their ideas and then to write down what they just said, or to rewrite a sentence in two or three other ways. They do that while I visit other students, and I return to check their work when they're done.

Whereas many grammar features can be discussed so as to emphasize the underlying principles that govern them, rules for prepositions and articles (which are nonexistent in a number of languages) are difficult to explain. These errors are more likely to diminish through students' long-term interaction with English than by direct instruction.

ANSWER KEY

This answer key is for activities in A Handbook for Writing. The activities in the handbook are noted with arrows. Answers will vary for most of the activities. Possible answers to some of the activities are listed here.

····▶ **Activity:** *Correcting punctuation errors in quotations* (page 254)

Here is one possible way to correct the punctuation errors in each sentence.

1. Kie Ho said in his article, "We Should Cherish Our Children's Freedom to Think," that while studying in Indonesia, he "simply did not have a chance to choose, to make decisions" whether to memorize or not "Hamlet's 'To be or not to be' soliloquy flawlessly" (page 113).

2. Students feel that they are being "stuffed with miscellaneous facts" (page 5). Because of this, they feel that they don't have enough time "to draw on [their] own resources, to use [their] own mind[s] for analyzing and synthesizing and evaluating this material" (page 5).

3. One student complained of being "so stuffed with miscellaneous facts, with such an indigestible mass of material, that he had no time (and was given no encouragement) to draw on his own resources, to use his own mind for analyzing and synthesizing and evaluating this material" (page 5).

····▶ **Activity:** *Analyzing sentence fragments* (pages 293–294)

The sample passage is taken from Antoine de Saint-Exupéry's *Flight to Arras*, a book about his experience as a pilot during World War II.

Sentence fragments:
"When there is no longer a place that is yours in the world."
"When you know no longer where your friend is to be found."

In sentences 3, 4, and 5, the structure begins with a simple subject-verb pattern: "The villagers come home . . . ," "The grain is stored . . . ," "The folded linen is piled. . . ." As sentence 6 tells us, ". . . each thing is in its place." The author's sentence structure reflects his theme. As the short, simple declarative sentences show, in time of peace everything is in a simple order, "in its place."

Sentence 9 acts as a transition to break that peace and order, beginning "Ah, but . . ." and telling us that "peace dies when the framework is ripped apart." Note that this sentence contains an independent and a dependent clause.

In sentences 10 and 11, the dependent clauses have been ripped away from their main clauses and stand alone as fragments. Again, the author's sentence structure reflects his theme. In time of war, life is fragmented.

Sentences become whole again (12 and 13) when peace is defined as the bringing together of parts to form a whole.

··· **Activity:** *Turning sentence fragments into sentences* (page 294)

1 I was pleased by the warm greeting I received from my American sponsor, whom I had also known from my previous job in Vietnam.

2 I disagree with Moore's argument that instructors' focus on self-esteem is connected to the problem of under-prepared students. The issue is much more complex than that.

3 Neusner and Harris both discuss college students, but they reveal different attitudes toward them, especially when it comes to the issue of how hard they work.

4 According to Barna, because the process of communicating across cultures can result in serious misunderstandings, the solution is to have an open mind.

5 Ho argues that freedom to think is an important component of education and that creativity is crucial as well.

··· **Activity:** *Correcting run-on sentences and comma faults* (page 294)

These answers show two possibilities for correction.

1 He would break everything down into pieces and start from scratch. He would then build on that slowly so that I would understand.

   He would break everything down into pieces and start from scratch, but he would then build on that slowly so that I would understand.

2 In the past, Americans had a tendency to think that English was the only language worth knowing and that foreigners were forced to learn it, so they did not even try to learn another language.

   In the past, Americans had a tendency to think that English was the only language worth knowing and that foreigners were forced to learn it. So they did not even try to learn another language.

3 However, the fact is that I am not a supernatural being. I could not take the stress.

   However, the fact is that I am not a supernatural being, and I could not take the stress.

4 My decision to apply early to college was meant to lighten the burden, but unfortunately, the three essays and several short questions added to my unbearable load.

   My decision to apply early to college was meant to lighten the burden. Unfortunately, the three essays and several short questions added to my unbearable load.

··· **Activity:** *Identifying clauses* (page 304)

1 Independent clause: *There's no doubt*

   Dependent clause: *that American education does not meet high standards in such basic skills as mathematics and language*

2 Dependent clause: *When I was 12 in Indonesia*

Dependent clause: *where education followed the Dutch system*

Independent clause: *I had to memorize the names of all the world's major cities, from Kabul to Karachi*

3 Independent clause: *I got*

Dependent clause: *so wild with rage that I seized the hurdle*

Independent clause: *and right before their eyes I smashed it to pieces*

4 Independent clause: *The most discouraging comment came from a professor*

Dependent clause: *who said he liked the passivity of students*

5 Independent clause: *I felt*

Dependent clause: *[that] I was making some progress in mastering the English language*

Dependent clause: *even if my collection of rejection slips seemed to shout otherwise*

⋯➤ Activity: *Correcting errors in clauses* (page 304)

1 The few who achieve complete insight and acceptance are outstanding by their rarity.

2 Though we rode several days inside of the iron horse, I do not recall a single thing about our luncheons.

3 I believed that her English reflected the quality of what she had to say.

4 This was the beauty for which I had always longed.

5 Despite your fantasies, it was not even that we wanted to be liked by you.

⋯➤ Activity: *Punctuating sentences* (page 327)

1 See the elephant eat Maria!
See the elephant. Eat, Maria.

2 Give the bird to my cousin Sylvia.
Give the bird to my cousin, Sylvia.

3 She said, "Hold it softly."
She said, "Hold it" (softly).

4 I can "can-can," but I can't cant. Can you?
– I can.
– Can can.
– But I can't.
– Can't?
– Can you?

PLANNING A WRITING COURSE

Guidelines allows for numerous possibilities for structuring a writing course. I include here three plans, each of which would need to be adapted to a particular classroom and time schedule. These plans are designed for a course that meets two to three times a week for fifteen weeks. I also include a thematic arrangement of readings in Appendix B.

Plan A

Plan A is for a course that uses every assignment in *Guidelines*, with the exception of library research. If there is too much work here, one of the assignments could be omitted and the work could be spread out over time.

Responding to Reading
Week 1
Strategies for Reading Critically
• "What True Education Should Do"/"Barriers"/"Waiting in Line at the Drugstore"
• Writing Workshop: Summarizing

Writing from Experience
Week 2
• "The School Days of an Indian Girl"/"My English"
• Writing Workshop: Making a List
• Writing Workshop: Freewriting and/or Looping

Week 3
• "College"/"A Book-Writing Venture"/"Mother Tongue"
• Writing Workshop: Cubing and/or Clustering Ideas for Writing
• Writing Workshop: Focusing Ideas/Structuring the Essay

Week 4
• Writing Workshop: Trial Draft of Essay #1
• Writing Workshop: Exchanging Feedback on Interim Draft of Essay #1

Week 5
• Writing Workshop: Revising/Locating Errors
• Revision of Essay #1 due

Relating Reading to Experience

Week 5, cont.
- "Intercultural Communication Stumbling Blocks"/"Social Time: The Heartbeat of Culture"
- Writing Workshop: Citing Ideas/Academic Integrity
- Writing Workshop: Paraphrasing

Week 6
- "Creativity in the Classroom"/"The Art of Reading"
- Writing Workshop: Quoting
- Writing Workshop: Exploring a Topic/Focusing Ideas/Structuring the Essay

Week 7
- Writing Workshop: Exchanging Feedback on Interim Draft of Essay #2

Analyzing an Argumentative Essay

Week 7, cont.
- "We Should Cherish Our Children's Freedom to Think"/"Teach Knowledge, Not 'Mental Skills'"
- Writing Workshop: Synthesizing

Week 8
- Revision of Essay #2 due
- "Grades and Self-Esteem"/"Confusing Harder with Better"/"The Commencement Speech You'll Never Hear"
- Writing Workshop: Exploring a Topic

Week 9
- Writing Workshop: Exchanging Feedback on Interim Draft of Essay #3

Analyzing Fiction

Week 9, cont.
- "The Ingrate"/"In the Land of the Free"
- Examining Elements of Fiction

Week 10
- Revision of Essay #3 due
- "America"/"Tito's Good-bye"/"Albert and Esene"
- Writing Workshop: Exploring a Topic

Week 11
- Writing Workshop: Exchanging Feedback on Interim Draft of Essay #4

Writing from Field Research

Week 11, cont.
- "Creativity in the Classroom"
- Selecting a Field Research Project

- Gathering Background Information
- Observing

Week 12
- Revision of Essay #4 due
- "The Relationship Between International and U.S.-Born Students: Two Perspectives"
- Interviewing/Conducting a Survey

Week 13
- In the field
- Writing Workshop: Methods/Results

Week 14
- Writing Workshop: Exchanging Feedback on Interim Draft of Essay #5

Week 15
- Revision of Essay #5 due
- Portfolio self-evaluation

Plan B

Plan B shows a plan for a course that focuses on writing from sources, including two different field research assignments.

Responding to Reading
Week 1
- Strategies for Reading Critically
- "What True Education Should Do"/"Barriers"/"Waiting in Line at the Drugstore"
- Writing Workshop: Summarizing

Relating Reading to Experience
Week 2
- "My English"/"Mother Tongue"/"College"
- Writing Workshop: Freewriting and/or Looping
- Writing Workshop: Citing Ideas/Quoting/Academic Integrity

Week 3
- "Intercultural Communication Stumbling Blocks"/"Social Time: The Heartbeat of Culture"
- Writing Workshop: Paraphrasing
- Writing Workshop: Exploring a Topic/Focusing Ideas/Structuring the Essay

Week 4
- Writing Workshop: Trial Draft of Essay #1
- Writing Workshop: Exchanging Feedback on Interim Draft of Essay #1
- Writing Workshop: Revising/Locating Errors

Analyzing an Argumentative Essay

Week 5
- Revision of Essay #1 due
- "We Should Cherish Our Children's Freedom to Think"/"Teach Knowledge, Not 'Mental Skills'"
- Writing Workshop: Synthesizing

Week 6
- "Grades and Self-Esteem"/"Confusing Harder with Better"/"The Commencement Speech You'll Never Hear"
- Writing Workshop: Exploring a Topic/Focusing Ideas/Structuring the Essay

Week 7
- Writing Workshop: Exchanging Feedback on Interim Draft of Essay #2
- Writing Workshop: Revising/Locating Errors

Writing from Field Research: Interviewing

Week 8
- Revision of Essay #2 due
- "Creativity in the Classroom"
- Selecting a Field Research Project
- Gathering Background Information
- Interviewing

Week 9
- In the field
- Writing Workshop: Methods/Results

Week 10
- Writing Workshop: Exchanging Feedback on Interim Draft of Essay #3
- Writing Workshop: Revising/Locating Errors

Writing from Field Research: Conducting a Survey

Week 11
- Revision of Essay #3 due
- "The Relationship Between International and U.S.-Born Students: Two Perspectives"
- Selecting a Field Research Project
- Gathering Background Information
- Conducting a Survey

Week 12
- In the field
- Writing Workshop: Methods/Results

Week 13
- Writing Workshop: Exchanging Feedback on Interim Draft of Essay #4
- Writing Workshop: Revising/Locating Errors

Week 14
- Revision of Essay #4 due
- "The Art of Reading"/"The Ingrate"

Week 15
- In-class Essay #5
- Portfolio self-evaluation

Plan C

Plan C shows a plan for a course that focuses on assignments for writing from sources, including a library research assignment.

Responding to Reading
Week 1
- Strategies for Reading Critically
- "What True Education Should Do"/"Barriers"/"Waiting in Line at the Drugstore"
- Writing Workshop: Summarizing

Relating Reading to Experience
Week 2
- "My English"/"Mother Tongue"/"College"
- Writing Workshop: Freewriting and/or Looping
- Writing Workshop: Citing Ideas/Quoting/Academic Integrity

Week 3
- "Intercultural Communication Stumbling Blocks"/"Social Time: The Heartbeat of Culture"
- Writing Workshop: Paraphrasing
- Writing Workshop: Exploring a Topic/Focusing Ideas/Structuring the Essay

Week 4
- Writing Workshop: Trial Draft of Essay #1
- Writing Workshop: Exchanging Feedback on Interim Draft of Essay #1
- Writing Workshop: Revising/Locating Errors

Analyzing an Argumentative Essay
Week 5
- Revision of Essay #1 due
- "We Should Cherish Our Children's Freedom to Think"/"Teach Knowledge, Not 'Mental Skills'"
- Writing Workshop: Synthesizing

Week 6
- "Grades and Self-Esteem"/"Confusing Harder with Better"/"The Commencement Speech You'll Never Hear"
- Writing Workshop: Exploring a Topic/Focusing Ideas/Structuring the Essay

Week 7
- Writing Workshop: Exchanging Feedback on Interim Draft of Essay #2
- Writing Workshop: Revising/Locating Errors

Writing from Library and Web-Based Research
Week 8
- Revision of Essay #2 due
- "Get in Line: The Extreme Shortage of ESL Classes"
- Selecting a Library and Web-Based Research Project
- Library Tour and Library Database Workshop

Week 9
- Conducting Web-Based Research
- Writing Workshop: Writing a Research Proposal
- Research Proposal due
- Exchanging Feedback on Research Proposals

Week 10
- Conducting Library Research
- Evaluating Sources
- Writing Workshop: Taking Notes on Research Sources

Week 11
- Writing Workshop: Writing a Progress Report
- Progress Report due
- Writing Workshop: Synthesizing
- Writing Workshop: Focusing Ideas/Writing a Preliminary Outline

Week 12
- Writing Workshop: Structuring the Essay
- Exchanging Feedback on Interim Draft of Essay #3
- Writing Workshop: Revising/Locating Errors

Week 13
- Oral Presentations of Research

Week 14
- Revision of Essay #3 due
- "Creativity in the Classroom"/"The Art of Reading"

Week 15
- In-class Essay #4
- Portfolio self-evaluation

THEMATIC ARRANGEMENT OF READINGS

The readings in *Guidelines* can be reorganized according to themes, several of which are listed below. Essay assignments could ask students to relate one or more readings within each theme to their own experience or to synthesize two or more readings within each theme. A final essay assignment could be a synthesis across two or more themes.

Communicating Across Languages and Cultures
"Barriers"
"The School Days of an Indian Girl"
"My English"
"A Book-Writing Venture"
"Mother Tongue"
"Intercultural Communication Stumbling Blocks"
"Social Time: The Heartbeat of Culture"

Teaching and Learning
"What True Education Should Do"
"The School Days of an Indian Girl"
"My English"
"College"
"Creativity in the Classroom"
"We Should Cherish Our Children's Freedom to Think"
"Teach Knowledge, Not 'Mental Skills'"
"Grades and Self-Esteem"
"Confusing Harder with Better"
"The Commencement Speech You'll Never Hear"
"The Ingrate"

Reading and Writing
"Waiting in Line at the Drugstore"
"My English"
"A Book-Writing Venture"
"Mother Tongue"
"The Art of Reading"
"The Ingrate"
"Albert and Esene"

Stories of Migration, Immigration, and Exile

"The School Days of an Indian Girl"

"My English"

"College"

"A Book-Writing Venture"

"Mother Tongue"

"The Ingrate"

"In the Land of the Free"

"America"

"Tito's Good-bye"

"Albert and Esene"

Oppression and Liberation

"Waiting in Line at the Drugstore"

"The School Days of an Indian Girl"

"The Ingrate"

"In the Land of the Free"

"Tito's Good-bye"